brilliant

Office Microsoft®

2007

POCKET BOOK

Jerri Ledford and
Rebecca Freshour

PEARSON

Prentice
Hall

Harlow, England • London • New York • Boston • San Francisco • Toronto • Sydney • Singapore • Hong Kong
Tokyo • Seoul • Taipei • New Delhi • Cape Town • Madrid • Mexico City • Amsterdam • Munich • Paris • Milan

Pearson Education Limited
Edinburgh Gate
Harlow CM20 2JE
Tel: +44 (0) 1279 623623
Fax: +44 (0) 1279 431059
Website: www.pearsoned.co.uk

First published in Great Britain in 2007

ISBN: 978-0-132-34059-5

British Library Cataloguing-in-Publication Data
A catalogue record for this book is available from the British Library.

10 9 8 7 6 5 4 3 2 1
11 10 09 08 07

Typeset in 10pt Helvetica Roman by 30
Printed and bound in Great Britain by Ashford Colour Press Ltd., Gosport

The Publisher's policy is to use paper manufactured from sustainable forests.

Brilliant Pocket Books

What you need to know – when you need it!

When you're working on your PC and come up against a problem that you're unsure how to solve, or want to accomplish something in an application that you aren't sure how to do, where do you look? If you are fed up with wading through pages of background information in unwieldy manuals and training guides trying to find the piece of information or advice that you need RIGHT NOW, and if you find that helplines really aren't that helpful, then Brilliant Pocket Books are the answer!

Brilliant Pocket Books have been developed to allow you to find the info that you need easily and without fuss and to guide you through each task using a highly visual step-by-step approach – providing exactly what you need to know, when you need it!

Brilliant Pocket Books are concise, easy-to-access guides to all of the most common important and useful tasks in all of the applications in the Office 2007 suite. Short, concise lessons make it really easy to learn any particular feature, or master any task or problem that you will come across in day-to-day use of the applications.

When you are faced with any task on your PC, whether major or minor, that you are unsure about, your Brilliant Pocket Book will provide you with the answer – almost before you know what the question is!

Brilliant Pocket Books Series

Series Editor: Joli Ballew

Brilliant Microsoft® Access 2007 Pocket Book *S.E. Slack*

Brilliant Microsoft® Excel 2007 Pocket Book *J. Peter Bruzzese*

Brilliant Microsoft® Office 2007 Pocket Book *Jerri Ledford & Rebecca Freshour*

Brilliant Microsoft® Outlook 2007 Pocket Book *Meryl K. Evans*

Brilliant Microsoft® PowerPoint 2007 Pocket Book *S.E. Slack*

Brilliant Microsoft® Windows Vista Pocket Book *Jerri Ledford & Rebecca Freshour*

Brilliant Microsoft® Word 2007 Pocket Book *Deanna Reynolds*

Contents

Overview of Word 2007   175

Introduction

Welcome to the *Brilliant Microsoft® Office 2007 Pocket Book* – a handy visual quick reference that will give you a basic grounding in the common features and tasks that you will need to master to use Microsoft® Office 2007 in any day-to-day situation. Keep it on your desk, in your briefcase or bag – or even in your pocket! – and you will always have the answer to hand for any problem or task that you come across.

Find out what you need to know – when you need it!

You don't have to read this book in any particular order. It is designed so that you can jump in, get the information you need and jump out – just look up the task in the contents list, turn to the right page, read the introduction, follow the step-by-step instructions – and you're done!

How this book works

Each section in this book includes foolproof step-by-step instructions for performing specific tasks, using screenshots to illustrate each step. Additional information is included to help increase your understanding and develop your skills – these are identified by the following icons:

 Jargon buster – New or unfamiliar terms are defined and explained in plain English to help you as you work through a section.

 Timesaver tip – These tips give you ideas that cut corners and confusion. They also give you additional information related to the topic that you are currently learning. Use them to expand your knowledge of a particular feature or concept.

 Important – This identifies areas where new users often run into trouble, and offers practical hints and solutions to these problems.

Brilliant Pocket Books **are a handy, accessible resource that you will find yourself turning to time and time again when you are faced with a problem or an unfamiliar task and need an answer at your fingertips – or in your pocket!**

Office 2007 Overview

1

Getting Started with Office 2007

In this lesson you'll learn about the new features that the Office 2007 application suite provides.

Microsoft Office 2007 is a full-service office productivity suite that consists of up to nine programs, depending on which edition you purchase:

■ Outlook (with Business Contact Manager): E-mail and contact management

■ Word: Word processing and document creation

■ Excel: Spreadsheet design and creation

■ PowerPoint: Presentation design and creation

■ Publisher: Publication design and creation

■ Access: Database design and creation

■ Groove: Virtual workspace creation, design and access

■ OneNote: Note-taking capabilities

■ InfoPath: Form design and creation.

The least inclusive edition is Home Office and Student 2007. This edition features only Word, Excel, PowerPoint and OneNote. The most inclusive edition is Microsoft Office Ultimate, which includes all of the programs in the list above. In addition to those programs, various versions could include other Microsoft programs, such as Microsoft Accounting Professional.

Microsoft has made significant changes to some of its Office programs. Once you learn to use them, however, you'll find they are now more efficient than in previous versions.

→ What's New in Office 2007

With Office 2007, Microsoft has created a whole new user interface for some programs that is much easier to use. The new interface includes the use of the *Office button*, which is located to the top left corner of the Document window, as shown in Figure 1.1, and takes the place of the file menu in previous versions. The *Quick Access Toolbar*, which is to the right of the Office button, can be customised and gives you quicker access to some of your most used menu commands. The most noticeable change of all, the *Ribbon*, organises commands into categories and gives you easier access to editing tools when and where you need them.

Figure 1.1
The tools of the new Office 2007 interface.

Though the new interface may, at first, seem daunting, it enables you to be more efficient when using Office 2007. And making it easier is what Office 2007 is all about.

→ Installing Office 2007

Before you buy Microsoft Office 2007, be sure that the program is compatible with your computer. It is recommended that you have at least 1 GB RAM with the Windows Vista Operating System. This is the minimum amount of RAM you should have, but having more is always better. You need a CD or DVD drive to install the operating system.

Follow these steps to install Microsoft Office 2007:

Important

Before you begin to install Office 2007 on your computer, be sure that you have backed up all of your important files and data. Because the operating system is being replaced, all of the files and programs that were operating on the old operating system will be erased.

1 Turn on your computer.

2 Insert the Office 2007 CD-ROM into your CD drive. The CD should automatically begin the installation process.

3 If the CD does not play automatically, select **Start > Run >** and type the letter of your CD drive followed by a colon (i.e. D:).

4 Once the disk begins to play, the Installation Wizard should appear on-screen. Follow the instructions provided in the wizard.

5 Once the installation is complete, restart your computer. When it has fully rebooted, you should have access to Office 2007.

Important

It could take more than an hour to complete the installation process and you'll have to restart your computer more than once during the process.

→ Activating and Registering Office

Once you have installed Office, you will have to activate and register the software before you can begin using it. To do this, you must have the registration code, which is located on the back of the package that the CD-ROM was in. The following steps are required to activate and register Office 2007:

1 During installation, you will be asked for the registration code from the software packaging. Copy that code **exactly** in the spaces provided when prompted.

2 Once the installation is finished, you will be prompted to register your software. Click to allow the connection over the Internet or to receive a telephone number which you can use to speak to Microsoft's customer services to activate and register your software.

3 When you've completed the registration process, Office 2007 is ready to use.

Important

You *will* be prompted to register your copy of Office 2007. Since Microsoft has cracked down on the use of illegal copies of its software, it is strongly recommended that you register the productivity suite immediately. If you have an active internet connection, registration will be much easier and will take far less time.

Once you have installed, activated and registered your Microsoft Office 2007 software, it is time to learn how to use it. The information in this book is designed to make that learning process as painless as possible.

2

Getting to Know Office 2007

In this lesson you'll learn how to open and navigate around Office 2007.

Before trying to use any new program, it's always a good idea to get to know your way around it first. Even if you have used the previous versions of Office, there have been enough changes to the user interface that it is a good idea to play around with it for a little while.

Rest assured that you can fix something if you don't like it. In Office 2007, you can go back to "the way things were" before you started experimenting, by pressing the keyboard combination **Ctrl + Z**. This will undo your last command.

Important

The **Ctrl + Z** combination works only for actions within a document or spreadsheet. If you make changes to the program (how it acts or how it looks), those changes cannot be undone with the **Ctrl + Z** combination.

→ Opening Office 2007

Follow these steps to open Office 2007:

1 Go to **Start > All Programs**.

2 Select **Microsoft Office**, as shown in Figure 2.1.

3 Then select the Office program you would like to open.

You can also open Office by double-clicking the icon on your desktop. If you do not have an icon on your desktop, click and drag the program for which you'd like a desktop shortcut from the All Programs menu to the desktop.

One additional way that you may be able to access your Office programs is through the Quick Start menu. When you click the Office button, a list of the most frequently used programs is displayed. If you've recently used one of the Office programs, it should appear on that menu. You can also pin that program to the

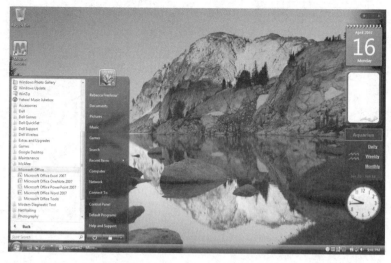

Figure 2.1
Locate your Office program menu in All Programs.

menu by right-clicking the program and selecting **Pin to Start Menu**. The program is then moved up above the dividing line in the Start menu and it will remain there until you "unpin" it.

You are now ready to start using Office 2007.

→ Exploring the New Workspace

As we pointed out in Chapter 1, some of the programs in Office 2007 have a new user interface. Exploring and getting to know the new interface is the first step to success in using Office. One change you should pay special attention to is the new Office button that replaced the file menu, as shown in Figure 2.2. It hasn't changed in all of the Office 2007 programs, however, so don't be surprised if you see the "old-fashioned" **File** menu in some of the programs (Publisher is one of them).

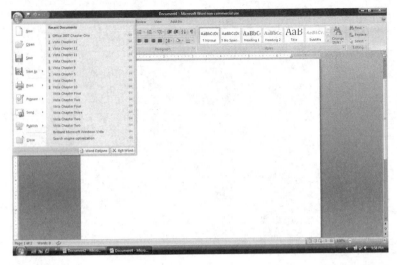

Figure 2.2
The Office button replaces the File menu in some Office programs.

The Office button gives you many of the same options that were available in the File menu of the past – saving, printing, opening and closing any document and even printing and publishing capabilities. If you let your pointer hover over the Office button (or any icon in the Ribbon), a tool tip appears with a brief description of what that icon or command is used for.

Navigating Office

To be able to navigate Office, you must be familiar with the new interface that's featured in some of the programs. Menus have been replaced by a Ribbon; there are contextual tabs that group together similar commands and some that appear when you need them most with commands that apply only to specific actions; and Styles and Galleries have been improved with Live Preview.

Using the Ribbon

The Ribbon, shown in Figure 2.3, is the most dramatic change to some of the Office programs. It replaces menus and toolbars in previous versions of Office. It is broken into categories called *contextual tabs*. Each tab displays a different group of commands for different types of actions. For example, in Word, the Home tab includes commands to change font, style, colour, bullets and numbering. The Review tab gives you the *review* options, such as Spelling and Grammar check, Word Count and the option to use the Office Thesaurus.

Figure 2.3
The Ribbon is the most notable interface change in some Office programs.

To use the Ribbon, choose the tab that has the commands you need and then select the command. If you are unsure what a command does, let your pointer hover over the command to show a tool tip with a brief description of what that command is used for, as shown in Figure 2.4. These are called *Screen Tips*.

Screen Tips give you the name of the command, the keyboard shortcut that you can use for the command and a short explanation of what it does. In some cases the Screen Tip may also include a picture of the function.

Figure 2.4
Screen Tips provide quick, helpful information.

Using the Contextual tabs

Contextual tabs are the tabs that you see above the Ribbon, as shown in Figure 2.5.

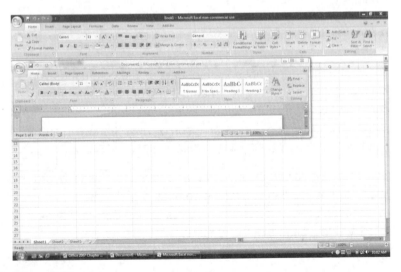

Figure 2.5
The contextual tabs group together similar actions for easier access.

Each contextual tab is a category of commands. To use the Ribbon, select the contextual tab that has the commands that you need. For example, if you wanted to view the print layout for a Word document, you would select the View tab. To insert a table or a picture, choose the Insert tab. Or for Spelling and Grammar check, choose the Review tab.

The Ribbon is actually much easier to use than the menus in previous Office programs. The contextual tabs group together functions in a manner that makes sense and since it's very visual, it's much easier to find the commands you seek. Not since the very first version has Office been this point-and-click easy.

Using Command Icons

Command icons are the small pictures that you see in each section of the Ribbon. These icons, shown in Figure 2.6, represent commands, or capabilities.

Figure 2.6
Command icons are graphical representations of available actions.

To use the commands, simply click the icon. In some cases, there is a menu behind an icon. This is indicated by a small downward-pointing arrow. Click the icon to expand the menu and then select options from the menu.

Using Styles and Galleries

When working in previous Office software, any time you wanted to use the Bold command, or change the colour or font of the text, you would have to take this step and that step and yet another step. If you wanted to use that same style again further in the document, you would have to go through the same steps as before. With Microsoft Office 2007, all but one of those monotonous steps have been removed using the Styles and Galleries menu.

The Styles and Galleries menu is located in the top right corner of the window of the Home Ribbon and says *Change Styles*. There is a downward-pointing arrow that opens a drop-down menu, as shown in Figure 2.7.

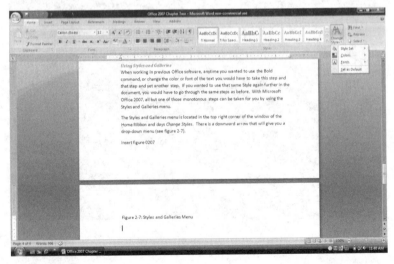

Figure 2.7
The Change Styles drop-down menu gives you additional style options.

You have four different options on the drop-down menu:

■ **Style Set**. When you select Style Set, you will see the Style Set Menu shown in Figure 2.8. This menu gives you several options to change the style of your document. If you let your pointer hover over each option, you can see the changes that style would make in your document without actually changing it. If you want to make the change permanent, click the style that you would like to use. These style changes are then applied to the whole document.

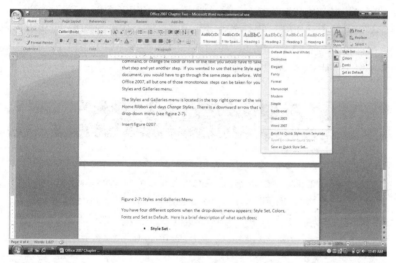

Figure 2.8
The Style Set menu lets you quickly make changes to the style of your whole document.

■ **Colors**. Choosing Colors from the Change Styles menu brings up a menu of colour schemes that you can choose from or gives you the option of making your own colour scheme. When you select a new colour scheme, it is applied to your entire document.

■ **Fonts**. This menu gives you several options for your font style. Once again, if you let your pointer hover over each font you can see the way your document will look before you actually choose to change it. If you decide to change your font, simply click the font that you would like to use and your font style changes throughout the entire document.

- ■ **Set as Default**. This option allows you to combine the styles you have used in one document and save them as the default option for styles.

Once you are familiar with the options to change the style of your documents, you can play around with them in a document and decide which are the most common styles that you will be using. You can then save them in the Gallery. By doing this, you create the option to choose that style for any future document. To apply a style from the Gallery, select the saved style from the Change Styles drop-down menu.

→ Using Live Preview

Several times throughout this chapter, we have made reference to holding your pointer over a certain change to see what that change would look like without having to actually commit to the change. This is called Live Preview. This new feature with Office 2007 allows you to preview changes before you actually make them.

To use Live Preview, take the following steps:

1 Place your cursor within the text of a document.

2 Go to the **Home** tab and select **Change Styles**.

3 Select the style change you would like to make and an expanded menu of style options appears.

4 Move your cursor from one option to the next in the expanded menu until you find the change that you like.

5 Once you find an option you like, click that option to make the change permanent. The change is immediately applied to your entire document.

The ability to change the style of an entire document with a single mouse-click is one of the most exciting (and most useful) features of Office 2007.

→ Finding Help

Regardless of how much you play in Office 2007, there is going to come a time when you will need to access the Help menu to answer a question. Office has an extensive Help menu that includes the option to search Microsoft Online to find additional answers to your questions.

To access the Help menu, select the question mark icon in the top right corner of an open program. This opens the help menu shown in Figure 2.9.

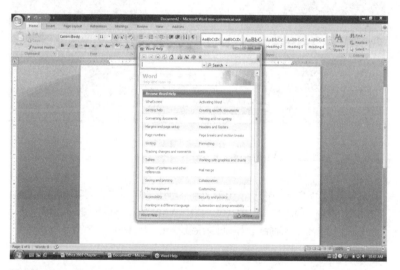

Figure 2.9
Microsoft Help menu.

Timesaver tip

You can also access Help by pressing the F1 key on your keyboard.

In the Help menu you can browse through topics or you can type a search query in the text box. Entering your search query in the text box may or may not produce an exact answer. You may have to browse through the results that appear. Keep in mind that if a word is spelled incorrectly, it may not be recognised.

Once you have found the topic that you are looking for, click the link to see the information about it. This often gives you several more headings from which to choose, as shown in Figure 2.10.

Figure 2.10
Use the Topic menu in Help to find the answers to your questions.

To see a previous subject that you have already viewed, click the back button. You can then return to what you were reading by clicking forward. Select the Home button to return to the main Help window.

When you are finished in Help, click the Close button to return to your previous activity.

3

Customising Office 2007

In this lesson you'll learn how to customise your Office applications.

→ Changing the Appearance of Office

There are several ways you can change the appearance of Office. The menu you see depends on which program you are working in, but getting to the menu in each program requires the same steps. To change the appearance of Office from any program, do the following:

1 Open the Office 2007 program you would like to change.

2 Click the **Office Button** (or **File** in some programs).

3 Select **Options**. This opens the Options dialogue box which contains several options for customising the program. For example, the Word Options dialogue box is shown in Figure 3.1.

4 Make the desired changes and then click **OK** to save the changes and return to the program you've been using.

Figure 3.1
The Options menu allows you to customise your Office applications.

For example, if you would like to customise your Word program, go into Word and choose Word Options from the file. Then select an area, such as Display, to change, as shown in Figure 3.2.

Figure 3.2
You can customise your display in Word.

This gives you three categories of options that you can customise. Make the changes that suit you and click **OK**. You can repeat this with all Options menus in each Office program.

Using Different Office Views

In each Office program, there is a View menu. This menu (it's a tab in some programs) allows you to change the way you view items and pages in Office. For an example, look at the **View** tab in Word, seen in Figure 3.3.

You have five options for the way you view a Word document:

■ **Print Layout**. This lets you see how a document will look when it is printed.

■ **Full Screen Reading**. This allows you to view the document or text in full screen without toolbars or taskbars or Ribbons. When you select Full Screen Reading, your document looks like an open book with two pages being displayed side by side. Arrows at the top of the window allow you to turn the pages forwards or backwards, as shown in Figure 3.4.

Figure 3.3
The View tab in Word allows you to change what and how you view documents.

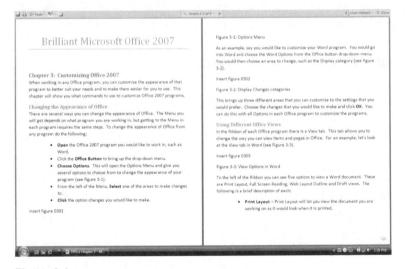

Figure 3.4
The Full Screen Reading view makes your document appear to be laid out like the pages of a book.

■ **Web Layout**. With this view you see the document as you would see a web page, as shown in Figure 3.5.

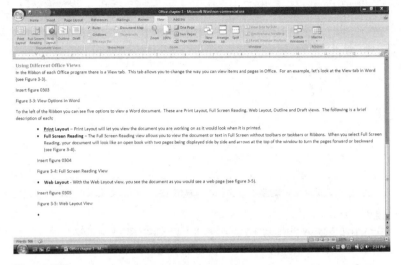

Figure 3.5
The web Layout view lets you see how your document would look on the web.

■ **Outline**. This shows you outlining tools while displaying the document as an outline, as shown in Figure 3.6. The Outline view works best when consistent headings and formatting have been applied throughout your document.

■ **Draft**. To help you to edit a document, you can view it in Draft view. With this view, shown in Figure 3.7, you can make revisions quickly. However, you will not be able to view headers, footers and some other elements of the text.

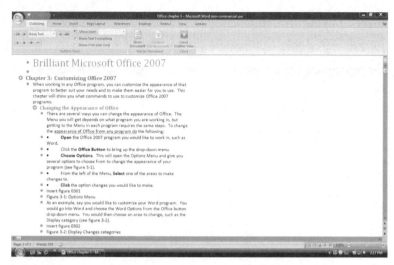

Figure 3.6
The Outline view shortens your document to an outline only.

Figure 3.7
The Draft view helps you to quickly edit drafts of your documents.

→ Customising Name, Initials and Language

Have you ever noticed that some Office documents seem to have an author's name and initials automatically attached to them? The author never thinks about doing this because the program does it automatically. If you would like to personalise your copy of Office 2007, follow these steps:

1 Click the **Office button**.

2 Select **Options**.

3 In the dialogue box that appears, look for a section that reads: **Personalize Your Copy of Microsoft Office**. In the text boxes provided, change the **User name** and **Initials** to match your own.

4 To change your default language, click the **Language Settings** button.

5 Once you have made the changes, select **OK** to save your changes and exit the menu.

→ Customising Ribbons and Toolbars

You cannot change the Ribbon in Office 2007 to look like previous toolbars and menus, but the Ribbon can be minimised to allow you more space to work. You can do this in one of two ways:

■ First, you can double-click the contextual tab on which you are working. This hides the Ribbon from view. When you're ready to use the Ribbon again, double-click the tab a second time.

■ Another way to hide the Ribbon is to select the down arrow next to the **Quick Access Toolbar** and choose **Minimize the Ribbon**. This hides the Ribbon and it stays hidden until you choose to show it again.

While you can't change the Ribbon, you *can* customise the Quick Access Toolbar by clicking the down-pointing arrow to the right of the toolbar, as shown in Figure 3.8.

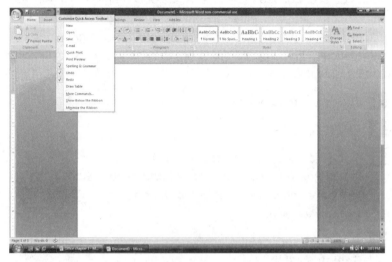

Figure 3.8
Use this menu to customise the Quick Access Toolbar.

When you look at the drop-down menu, the items that have checkmarks beside them are the items that show on your Quick Access Toolbar. If you do not want them to appear on the Quick Access toolbar, click to remove the checkmark. If there is something that is not checked that you would like to see on the toolbar, click the box beside it to select it, which adds it to the toolbar. You can select Popular Commands to see other items that you can add to the toolbar, as shown in Figure 3.9.

Notice that you can also choose to move the Quick Access Toolbar below the Ribbon if you prefer to have it there.

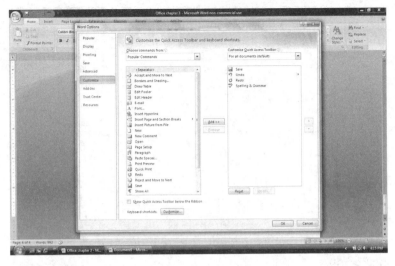

Figure 3.9
More Quick Access Toolbar options.

→ Creating Custom AutoCorrect Entries

At one time or another, we are all grateful for AutoCorrect. Here you are, typing along just as fast as you can, and you spell a word wrong, but thanks to AutoCorrect you don't have to stop, go back and change the word. Did you know, however, that you can create custom entries for AutoCorrect?

Use these steps to create custom entries for AutoCorrect:

1 Click the Office button.

2 Choose **Word Options**.

3 Select **Proofing** from the menu on the left side of the customisation dialogue box, as shown in Figure 3.10.

4 Next, select **AutoCorrect Options**. The AutoCorrect dialogue box appears.

Figure 3.10
Use the Proofing menu to access AutoCorrect Options.

5 On the AutoCorrect tab use the **Replace**: _____ **With**: _____ section, as shown in Figure 3.11, to create an entry. Type the frequently misspelled word in the **Replace**: _____ section of the phrase and the correct word in the **With**: _____ section of the phrase.

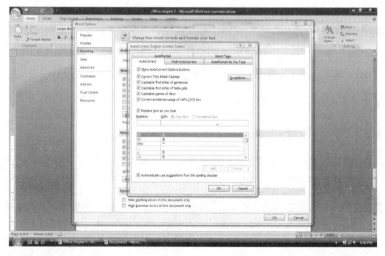

Figure 3.11
The AutoCorrect Options dialogue box is where you add entries.

6 Click **Add** and repeat with any other entries that you want to add.

7 When you have added all the entries you want, click **OK** to return to the **Word Options** dialogue box and **OK** to close out of it.

Now your custom AutoCorrect entries have been added.

4

Creating Office Users and Groups

In this lesson you'll be introduced to users and groups and learn how to configure user and group permissions as well as manage project data.

→ Understanding Users and Groups

An important consideration for many people who work on a network is the process of authorising users, groups and computers to access documents and files on the network. This is sometimes called access control. Controlling access in Office 2007 is accomplished by granting permissions to different users and groups of users.

There are a lot of technical details about how all of this works, but that's not necessarily what's important. What is important is understanding how to configure users and groups and how to grant permissions to those groups. It's not a difficult task once you get the hang of it.

→ Configuring User and Group Permissions

Before you can grant permissions for a file to users or groups, you must establish who the owner of the document or file is. The owner is the person who controls how permissions are set for the document or file. That owner is usually your network administrator, since they are responsible for network servers and the files and applications on those servers. But you don't have to be a network administrator to be able to grant permissions to other users or groups of users.

Setting permissions isn't nearly as complicated as it all sounds. Follow these steps to grant permissions to a file or document to other users or groups of users:

1 Navigate to the file or folder that you want to enable permissions for. Right-click on it.

2 Click Properties. The Properties dialogue box appears.

3 Select the Security tab, as shown in Figure 4.1.

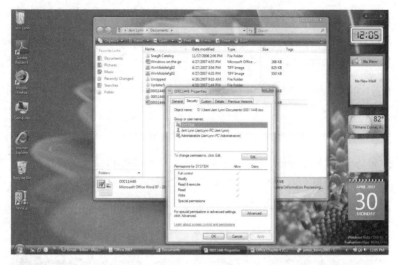

Figure 4.1
Use the security tab of the Properties dialogue box to add permissions.

4 To set permissions for a new group or user, click **Add**.

5 Enter the requested information in the Select Users, Computers, or Groups window, then click **OK**.

There are some aspects to consider as you assign permissions. You can control user access by granting, changing, or denying permissions for individuals and groups. Some things to remember about permissions:

■ File and folder permissions can only be set on drives formatted to use New Technology File System (NTFS). This is the new default file management system in Microsoft Windows.

■ Owners or administrators can change permissions, but so can users who have been granted permissions by the owner or administrator. Use caution when granting file permissions and grant permissions only to those you trust.

■ By default, new users and groups have permission to Read & Execute, List Folder Contents, and Read. If you want users to have more permissions, you have to grant them individually.

Deleting Permissions for Files and Folders

To change or remove permissions from existing groups or users, follow these steps:

1 Right-click the document for which you would like to revoke permissions.

2 Select **Properties** and the **Properties** dialogue box appears.

3 On the **Security** tab, highlight the name of the group or user for which you want to remove permissions.

4 Select **Edit** and the **Permissions** dialogue box appears, as shown in Figure 4.2.

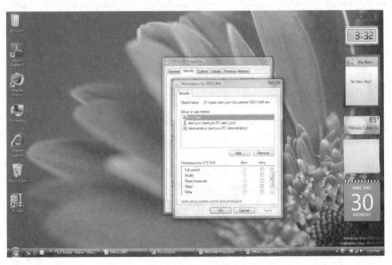

Figure 4.2
Use the Permissions dialogue box to edit permissions.

5 Place checkmarks next to the permissions you would like to deny, or click **Remove** to remove the user or group completely.

6 When finished, click **Apply** and then **OK** to return to the **Properties** dialogue box.

7 Click **Apply** and then **OK** to close the dialogue box and save your changes.

→ Managing Project Data

Office 2007 has some great new features for document and records management. For example, you can restrict sensitive information from being forwarded, copied, or printed. That protection remains with the file or document no matter where it is accessed from.

In order for a user to open a restricted document or file, they must connect to a licensing server, which requires a user licence to be downloaded and installed. The process verifies users' credentials using information about their e-mail address and permission rights. Without going through the verification process and receiving a user licence, the file cannot be opened.

In order to use these data management features, you must have Windows Rights Management Services Client Service Pack 1. You can download the file from the Microsoft Online website (www.microsoft.com/downloads/details.aspx?familyid= a154648c-881a-41da-8455-042d7033372b&displaylang=en) or if you receive a file that has been protected, Office 2007 prompts you to download it if it doesn't already exist on your computer.

5

Collaborating with Others

In this lesson you'll learn about SharePoint Services and Groove 2007.

→ Understanding SharePoint Services

When you hear the term SharePoint Services, it sounds a little daunting. What in the world is this and why should I care? In simple terms, Windows SharePoint Services is part of Windows Server 2003 and uses a browser-based workspace technology to help people collaborate.

Office SharePoint Server 2007 is a suite of server-based applications that connects sites, people and business processes. You may or may not use these two technologies. Most businesses that have an IT department do, but if you're an individual, you may not even have need of these services.

If you do have it, SharePoint Services lets you create websites that teams can use to share information and for document collaboration. The resources available on these websites include portals, team workspaces, e-mail, calendar viewing, presence awareness and web-based conferencing.

There are many books available to help you learn more about SharePoint Services or SharePoint Server. They can be complicated to use and there just isn't enough space in this book to cover all of the details that you need to know.

→ Understanding Groove 2007

Another collaborative effort from Microsoft is Groove 2007. Groove is an environment that puts team members, communications, tools and information together in one location that is accessible by each of the team members.

To invite people to share a workspace in Groove, follow these steps:

1 On the Groove launchbar, double-click the file-sharing workspace on the Workspaces tab.

2 In the Synchronization Tasks pane, select Invite.

3 Then select recipient and role options in the Send Invitation dialogue box.

It doesn't matter where a team member might be located, because the actual workspace is stored on the team member's individual computer and synchronised when the team member accesses the Internet or corporate network. It is necessary for all team members to have Groove 2007 installed on their computers, however.

Groove 2007 includes several options for workspaces. You can select the one that fits your personal needs and then invite other people to join you. These options include:

■ Standard workspace: This space includes files and discussion tools. But you can add tools if needed.

■ File-sharing workspace: This workspace allows you to synchronise a selected file folder and its contents across participating computers. Everything within the file (which is usually an operating system file) is synchronised on all computers, so everyone stays up to date.

■ Template workspace: In this space, you select from several options designed to meet project requirements. These options include capabilities such as a calendar or sketchpad for collaborating on dates and drawings.

When someone you've invited accepts the invitation you sent them to the Groove workspace, an exact copy of it is placed on their desktop. And it's not necessary for those people to be on the same network as you – you can collaborate with people on other networks, even if they are halfway around the world.

To invite people to a file-sharing workspace:

1 Double-click the file-sharing workspace on the Workspaces tab of the Groove launchbar.

2 Click Invite Someone in the Synchronization Tasks pane.

3 Select recipient and role options in the Send Invitation dialogue box.

Overview of Outlook 2007

6

Using Outlook 2007

In this lesson you'll be introduced to the new features in Outlook 2007 and learn how to navigate around it.

→ What's New in Outlook 2007

Outlook has changed very little in its appearance since its initial release in 1997. Its functionality, however, continues to improve and Outlook 2007 is no disappointment in terms of new features.

Here are some of the feature enhancements in Outlook 2007:

■ Instant Search: Every window contains an Instant Search box to allow you to find messages, contacts and appointments quickly.

■ Junk mail filters: The filters have been improved in 2007, with a new phishing filter to protect you from scammers.

■ To-Do List: Located to the right of the main window, you now can see a list of everything you need to do for that day (or other times you select). It contains a calendar, appointments are mapped out for you and they can be colour coded for easier reference.

■ New Ribbon interface: The main window doesn't have the new Ribbon, but the message interface does.

■ Attachment preview: Allows you to see what is in an attachment (for most file types) without having to open another program to launch it.

■ RSS feed support: You can now read blog site information that has RSS format. (For an explanation of RSS, see Chapter 15.)

These are some of the more prominent features that are available in Outlook 2007 (see Figure 6.1). The interface, overall, is sleeker and allows for much more than a simple e-mail tool would offer, but provides an entire organising tool, for either your life or your business.

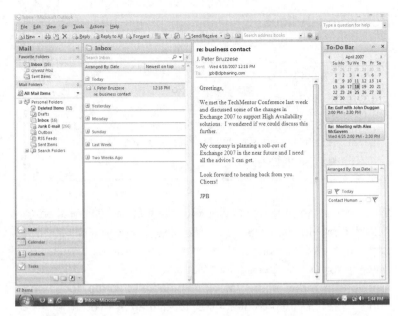

Figure 6.1
A look at the new Outlook 2007.

→ Starting Outlook

Opening Outlook for the first time is straightforward but differs slightly depending on whether you are using XP or Vista as your operating system.

If you are using XP, you need to select the Start button, then Programs and locate your Microsoft Office folder and select Outlook 2007 (unless you have it in your Quick launchbar or located right at the Start menu).

If you are using Vista, you can select the Windows button and type Outlook in your search bar to locate the program. Then hit Enter. (In addition, you can launch it from your Quick launchbar or from the Start menu if it is located there.)

Activating Outlook

When you attempt to use Outlook for the first time you will be asked to provide a product key. Without this key you will still be allowed to use Outlook for a specific period of time (default is 25 days). After the trial period your Outlook will go into a reduced functionality mode where you won't be able to create documents and so forth. If you provide the key it will then ask you whether you want to activate the software. You can do this either through the Internet (the easier method) or over the phone.

If you didn't activate Outlook when you started the program the first time you can still activate by selecting Help and then Activate Product. If the product was already activated you will receive a message informing you that the product is activated.

→ Customising Outlook

There are three primary areas you might want to customise: the Navigation pane, the To-Do Bar and the Reading Pane. Let's consider ways to customise each of these.

The Navigation pane

Located on the left-hand side of the Outlook window, there are seven navigation buttons you can select: Mail, Calendar, Contacts, Tasks, Notes, Folder List and Shortcuts.

You can customise the Navigation pane in the following ways:

■ You can expand or shrink the list of navigation buttons by raising or lowering the handle located above the Mail button. If you shrink it, those buttons will become mini-buttons at the bottom of the pane, as shown in Figure 6.2.

■ If you want to add or remove buttons from the list, you right-click any of the buttons and select "Navigation pane Options" (also shown in Figure 6.2). You will be able to select or clear checkboxes.

■ From within the Navigation pane Options you can also select the Move Up or Move Down options to alter the location of the button in the Navigation pane.

■ Notice there are double arrows (>>) pointing in a variety of directions which indicate your ability to expand or shrink certain panes. For example, if you want to minimise the Navigation pane you can select the << arrow to minimise it to the left side wall.

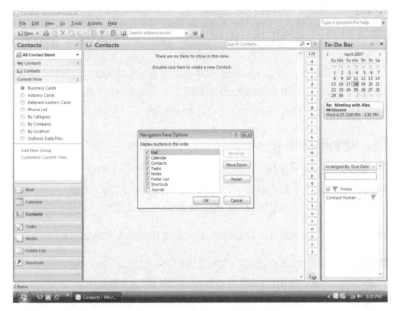

Figure 6.2
Customising the Navigation pane options.

Timesaver tip

You can drag any program shortcut to the Shortcuts list to give you one-click access to that program. If you are using Windows Vista, however, you may receive warning messages when trying to open certain programs in this way, as part of newer security features. You can also drag web page shortcuts to the Shortcuts list. If selected, the web page will open up within the Outlook window.

Another way you can alter the view of the Navigation pane is through the View menu selection. If you select View and then Navigation pane, you can choose one of the following: Normal, Minimized, Off. You can also turn off the Navigation pane by typing **Alt+F1**.

The To-Do Bar

Like the Navigation pane, you can alter the view of the To-Do Bar by selecting the side double arrows (>>) to minimise the bar. Or you can select View and then To-Do Bar and you can choose Normal, Minimized or Off. You can also turn off the To-Do Bar by typing **Alt+F2**.

In addition, you can turn features of the To-Do Bar on and off. These include the Date Navigator (which is really just your calendar), the Appointments and the Task List. This is done through the View – To-Do Bar selection. There is a final setting called Options, as shown in Figure 6.3. From here you can determine the number of months shown (the default is 1) and the number of appointments (the default is 3).

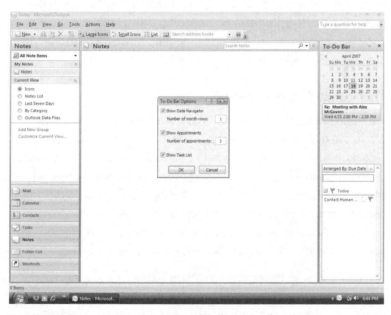

Figure 6.3
To-Do Options.

The Reading Pane

The Reading Pane will show you the contents of the item that is currently selected. You can place the Reading Pane at the right or bottom of the Outlook window by selecting **View > Reading Pane** and then choose Right, Bottom or Off. By default it is located at the right which is believed to be the location that allows you to be the most productive.

Toolbars and the Status Bar

You can also customise the toolbars you have displayed in Outlook by selecting **View > Toolbars** and then selecting or de-selecting the available toolbars.

The Status Bar is located at the bottom of your screen. It will display information about the status (or number) of items in the main window, the progress of a specific task or the current condition of a program. It is on by default, however from the View menu you can select it to turn it off if you prefer.

The Quick Access Toolbar

Although Outlook 2007 doesn't have the new ribbon interface within the main window, creating new messages reveals that the Message window does include the new interface. Unlike toolbars, ribbons cannot be altered by users. You cannot add or remove which ribbons you want or change the options available on certain ribbons. However, at the top of the message window is the Quick Access Toolbar, as shown in Figure 6.4, where you can add any command you want for easy and speedy access.

You can see from the figure that if you select the down-pointing arrow next to the toolbar, you have the ability to choose additional command buttons to be placed on the toolbar (or remove those you do not need). You can also choose to have the Quick Access Toolbar placed below the ribbon. Or you can select the "Minimize the Ribbon" option if you want to free up some more space by reducing the ribbons to just their tabs.

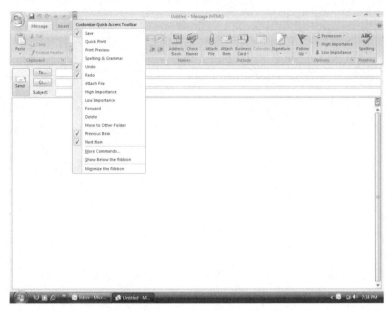

Figure 6.4
The Quick Access Toolbar.

If you select "More Commands" from the Quick Access customisation down-pointing arrow (as shown in Figure 6.5), you will be given the opportunity to add just about any command or macro that Outlook has.

Timesaver tip

The Quick Access Toolbar can really help you save time because you can bring all your favourite options to one location. To make it easier to reach, we recommend you change the settings so the toolbar is below your ribbons and make sure you add all the buttons you need or want. Being below the ribbon gives the toolbar plenty of room to grow.

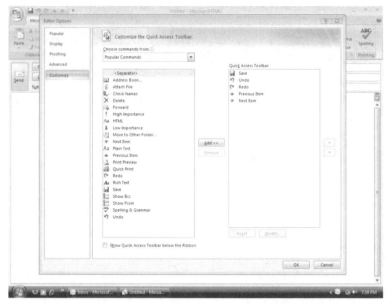

Figure 6.5
Adding more commands to the Quick Access Toolbar.

→ Navigating Around Outlook 2007

Outlook 2007 is one of those tools that 50 years ago would have left people reeling in amazement. Why? Because when you think about it, in addition to sending and receiving mail, it allows you to organise your schedule, manage contacts, take notes, hook into RSS feeds... it even reminds you when you have a meeting (or golf appointment, whichever you prefer).

With so much functionality comes the complication of use. It may take a while to get used to all of the screens and options at your disposal. If you are new to Outlook and want to get used to the e-mail side first, then turn off the To-Do Bar to remove the eye clutter from your screen. You can turn it back on once you are comfortable.

To navigate into a different aspect of the program, use the navigation buttons from the Navigation pane. These will bring you to the programs window where you can begin to get comfortable with each aspect.

To learn more about the message interface, select the **New** button from the main window. This will bring up a new message template where you can see the various ribbons you have to work with. Select a ribbon tab to take you to the next set of functions.

→ Creating a New Profile in Outlook

Do you know people who have more than one e-mail account? Maybe they have a Gmail account and a Yahoo account and a Hotmail account. With these accounts they may check their e-mail online, or they might use their Internet web browsers to check mail.

You may have these web-based accounts. Or you may use Outlook in your company through an e-mail server (possibly called an exchange server, if the e-mail server is running Microsoft software). You might have SMTP/POP3/IMAP accounts as well. In every case Outlook 2007 can be the connecting point between you and your mail. All you have to do is configure your profile.

Jargon buster

Profiles include all your user account settings for your e-mail. These settings include your name and e-mail address. Depending on the type of account, you may have to include information such as the POP3 or SMTP mail server you are using and passwords for your account.

You can create your profile in one of the following ways:

■ The first time you run Outlook a wizard will begin the process of creating an initial profile and will walk you through the various settings you need to configure.

■ If you are working within a company, your Outlook profile might already have been established by your network administrator who would configure your Outlook to work with the in-house exchange server.

■ From within **Control Panel**, under the Mail applet you can choose the type of account you want and then proceed to the Auto Account Setup dialogue.

■ If you are working in Outlook and have a profile but wish to make changes, you can select the **Tools** menu, then **Account Settings**. From the **E-mail** tab you select **New** and choose the type of account you want and then proceed to the **Auto Account Setup** dialogue boxes.

We went through those options a bit fast. Let's slow it down a bit and step through the process. To create a new user profile, perform the following:

1 If you want to use **Control Panel**, open the Mail applet. Select **E-mail Accounts** and this will take you to the Account Settings dialogue, shown in Figure 6.6. (Or, from within Outlook itself, select the **Tools** menu, then select **Account Settings**.)

Timesaver tip

If you already know that you are going to be configuring an account to work with an exchange server, use the Control Panel > Mail approach to configuring your settings. If you try to configure an exchange account while in Outlook, you will be told to close Outlook and establish the account through the Control Panel > Mail settings.

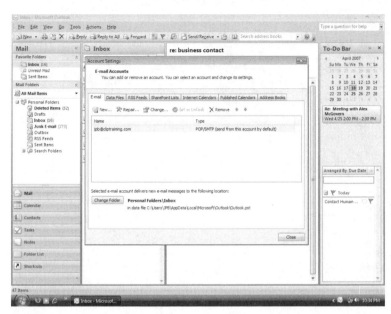

Figure 6.6
The Account Settings dialogue for creating user profiles.

2 Select **New** and you will be presented with two radio buttons under the Choose E-mail Service dialogue. One asks whether you want to use Microsoft Exchange, POP3, IMAP, or HTTP. The other offers Other services like Fax Mail Transport and Outlook Mobile Services. Usually you will select the former and then **Next**.

3 The **Auto Account Setup** dialogue appears, as shown in Figure 6.7. From here you need to add your name, e-mail address and password for the account. If you select **Next**, Outlook will automatically attempt to determine your correct server settings (using some standard methods based upon your e-mail address). If the servers are configured in a traditional way, this should work fine. Otherwise you may have to manually configure your servers. If not, your profile will be created and you will be ready to read/write and send mail.

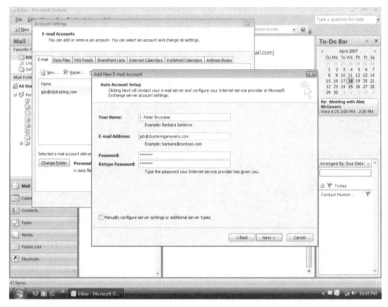

Figure 6.7
The Auto Account Setup dialogue.

If you already know you need to (or simply want to) configure your servers manually, you can select the checkbox "Manually configure server settings or additional server types".

4 If you choose to manually configure your settings you will be presented with the option to **Choose Your E-mail Service**. Your options include the following:

a   Internet E-mail: Connect to your POP, IMAP, or HTTP server to send and receive e-mail messages.

b   Microsoft Exchange: Connect to Microsoft Exchange for access to your e-mail, calendar, contacts, faxes and voice mail.

c   Other: Connect to a server type shown below. Fax Mail Transport or Outlook Mobile Services (Text Messaging).

5 Select Internet E-mail. You will be taken to the Internet E-mail Settings dialogue, shown in Figure 6.8. Provide your name and e-mail address. Select an account type (POP, IMAP or HTTP). Then configure your incoming and outgoing mail servers. (Note: if you aren't 100% sure, you can take a guess with POP or SMTP with the last part of your e-mail at the end. So, if your e-mail is lmh@cliptraining.com, it's possible that your servers will be pop.cliptraining.com and smtp.cliptraining.com. If this doesn't work, you will have to contact your Internet service provider (or e-mail administrator) to provide you with the proper server settings. Finally, provide a user name and password for the account (this should be one that is already established, either by you or by your e-mail administrator).

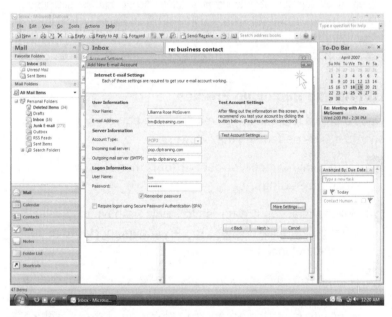

Figure 6.8
The Internet E-mail Settings dialogue (with filled-in settings).

6 At this point you can choose one of the following:

a Test Account Settings: Select this button if you want to ensure the functionality of your new account.

b More Settings: Allows you to make changes in the port numbers that POP and SMTP use, authentication settings for your SMTP server if it is different from your POP server, connection methods and so forth.

c Select "Next" to finish the account profile creation.

Important

Configuring your exchange e-mail settings is beyond the scope of this book. Typically your network administrator will configure these settings for you or provide you with clear, step-by-step instructions on how to configure them.

Editing and Removing Profiles

Once a profile is created, you may need to edit or remove it. You can do this by performing the following:

1 From within Outlook, select the **Tools** menu and then **Account Settings**.

2 Select the account you wish to edit (or remove) and select **Change** (to make changes to the account) or **Remove** (to remove the account).

3 Note, if you have more than one profile, you can set one as the default account. You can also use the **Up and Down** arrows to move the accounts to higher and lower positions within the **E-mail Settings**. This will change which accounts get checked for e-mail first (based upon whichever account is higher in the list).

7

Sending and Receiving E-mail in Outlook 2007

In this lesson you'll get an introduction to creating, sending, responding to and forwarding e-mails. You'll also learn how to work with the Address Book and Reading Pane.

→ An Introduction to E-mail

Most of the world is familiar with e-mail at this point, but there are always newcomers. They have finally decided to leave behind traditional mail (often called snail mail by the cyber crowd) and venture into immediate communication. Once you master the world of e-mail you will have to adjust to a whole new vernacular (one that uses ;-) to smile and wink at you, or LOL to indicate "laugh out loud"). You will have e-cards sent to you by friends, you will receive forwarded news events and cute stories, or pictures of hearts and hugs. On the downside, you will also receive spam and phishing e-mails.

Jargon buster

Spam is unsolicited messages that are usually sent in bulk. It's junk e-mail (similar to when you receive unsolicited junk mail in your real mailbox). Why the word spam? According to en.wikipedia.org, supposedly it originated with early chat rooms. When an individual would enter a chat room and strike up unwanted conversations, people would type the Monty Python "Spam" skit (which goes something like "Spam, Spam, Spam, Eggs," etc…) which would make communication impossible, until the unwanted guest left the room.

Phishing is worse than spam. It's actually a social engineering method to get people to give away personal information such as user names and passwords to their banking or other accounts. A social engineer is a modern day con artist who tricks people, in the case of phishing, by sending an e-mail that looks like it is really from your bank or other vendor. It may lead you to a website that looks correct but is actually a fake. Happily, Outlook 2007 has a phishing filter to help protect you, although you have to be on guard personally for these types of tricks.

All in all, e-mail is an excellent way to communicate quickly (and more dynamically) with both business contacts and loved ones around the world.

→ Creating and Sending E-mail

In Outlook 2007, to begin the process of creating an e-mail, the quickest way from the main window is to have the Mail navigation button selected (as opposed to Calendar or Contacts or one of the other options) and to select the New button in the top, left-hand corner of the main window. This will open a message template.

Timesaver tip

If you happen to be working in your Calendar or one of the other applications, you can open a message template by selecting the down arrow next to the "New" button, in the top, left-hand corner of the main window. From the list you want to select Mail Message.

Once you have a mail template open you need to perform the following steps to complete your e-mail before sending:

1 Much like a real letter, you need to decide who you are sending the letter to and add that e-mail address (or addresses) into the To part of the template. For example, if you have a friend who has the e-mail address marionjones@silverstar.com you can type this address in the To bar, as shown in Figure 7.1.

2 If you want to add more people to your e-mail, so that it goes to more than one person, you can add a semi-colon (;) between e-mail addresses. You can also add more addresses to the Cc portion of your template.

Jargon buster

Cc stands for carbon copy, which is what it used to be called to make a copy of a document using carbon paper to produce the copy.

3 Once you have inserted all the e-mail addresses you plan to send this message to in the To or Cc boxes, you need to provide a Subject. You can just type in something like "Welcome to the Company!" or whatever else you choose. However, many people include "re:" to introduce the subject, for example, "Re: Our Meeting Next Week".

Jargon buster

Re: is commonly thought to mean "regarding" and in the case of e-mail that is somewhat accurate. However, it is actually from Latin meaning "in the matter of".

4 The next step is composing the body of your message. On the Message ribbon you have the ability to format your message in any way you like. You can change the font type, colour and size. You can bold, indent or underline text or align the text differently on the page, and more.

5 Once your message is ready, your final step is to select the large **Send** button.

Respond and Forward

It's important to note that there are other ways to create an e-mail. For example, when you receive an e-mail, you can select one of the following buttons:

■ Reply: This will reply to the person who sent you the e-mail. Their e-mail address will automatically be placed in the To location.

■ Reply to All: This will reply to the person who sent you the e-mail, along with everyone else noted in the sender's To, Cc and Bcc options.

■ Forward: This allows you to take the e-mail you received from someone else and forward it to anyone else you choose.

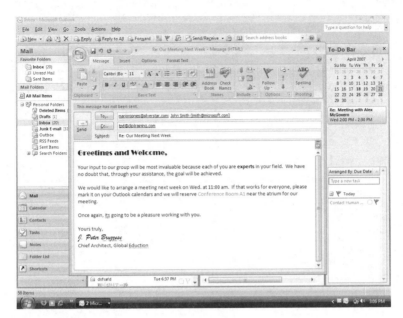

Figure 7.1
Filling in all the parts of an e-mail message before sending.

You can find these buttons in two locations. One is within your main window, when your Mail navigation pane is open. You can select an e-mail without opening it and select the Reply, Reply to All, or Forward buttons from the top toolbar. Or you can open a message you have received and select the Reply, Reply to All or Forward buttons from the Message ribbon, under the Respond grouping, as shown in Figure 7.2.

Changing the Message Format

When you compose an e-mail, by default the mail template uses an HTML format. You can also use Plain Text or Rich Text. Let's review each of these formats and how to alter the format used for your messages.

■ Plain Text: Transmits only letters and numbers. Any formatting, including colours, fonts and pictures, is removed.

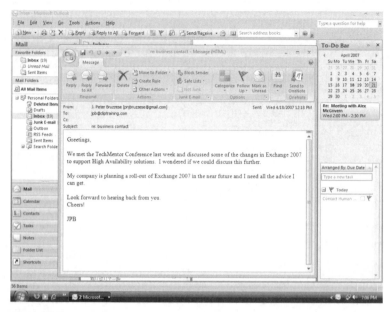

Figure 7.2
Reply, Reply to All and Forward options.

■ Rich Text: This format was used before HTML was popular and is able to use formatting within the messages. The problem is that only users of Outlook will be able to see your message in the proper way. So this is fine if you are using e-mail within a company that uses an exchange server.

■ HTML: Offers the same abilities as Rich Text format but goes further by allowing you to use different styles, add graphics as background images and more. Modern e-mail applications can read HTML messages.

To change the message format for an individual message, perform the following:

1 Begin a new e-mail. From within the message template, select the **Options** ribbon.

2 Under the Format grouping you can choose Plain Text, HTML, or Rich Text.

If you want to change the message format used for the default e-mail you create, you can alter the settings by performing the following:

1 From the main window, select **Tools**, then **Options**.

2 Go to the **Mail Format** tab, shown in Figure 7.3.

3 Under the Message Format settings, select the down arrow to choose one of the message format types for all new e-mails.

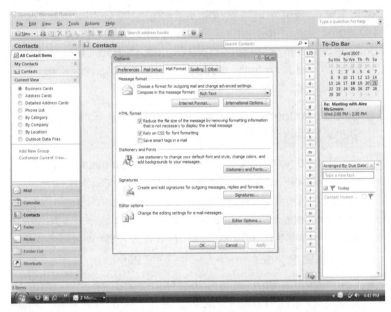

Figure 7.3
Changing the Message Format.

→ Working with the Address Book

Have you ever forgotten an e-mail address? Or typed in an e-mail manually only to realise that you mistyped the e-mail and it went to the wrong person? This happens all too often, which is why the best approach to e-mail address management is your Address Book.

The Address Book is not one specific folder but in Outlook 2007 it actually pulls its information from folders on your system that have contact information in them. This is quite beneficial because you can structure your contact information in multiple folders (such as Business and Home) and separate your contacts.

Creating Some Contacts

The first thing you need to do is add entries into the Address Book. The easiest way to do this is through the Contacts portion of Outlook. The simple form that you fill out makes adding new contacts a simple process. We will discuss the Contacts tool in Chapter 14, but for a quick introduction on adding contacts, perform the following:

1 Select the **Contacts** navigation button from within your Outlook main window.

2 If you have no contacts yet there will be a message in the main window saying "Double-click here to create a new Contact". Double-click to open up the Contact form template, shown in Figure 7.4. Or you can select the **New** button in the top, left-hand corner of the main window and you will be brought to the Contact template.

3 Complete the form fields to the degree you are able (or for simplicity, provide the name and e-mail of the person). When it is complete, select the **Save & Close** button located on the Contact ribbon, under the **Actions** grouping.

Using the Address Book

There are different ways to work with the Address Book. The first way is through the main window on the Standard toolbar. Click the Address Book button to display the information you placed in your Contacts folder, as shown in Figure 7.5. This allows you to search for contacts for which you want to modify information, or to whom you would like to send a message. To send a message you need to find the contact, double-click their name and enter the contact form

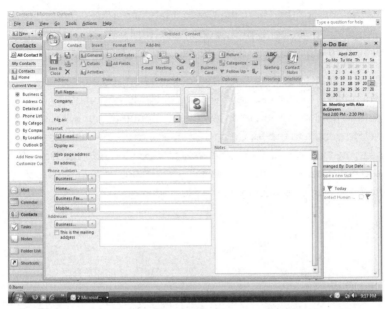

Figure 7.4
Fill in a name and e-mail in the Contact form template.

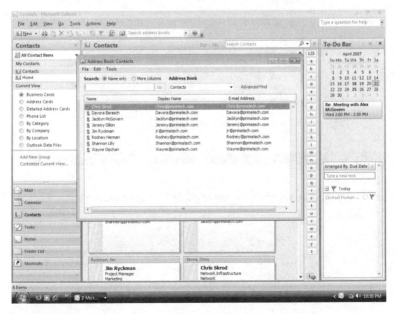

Figure 7.5
Using the Address Book to search for contacts.

for the person. Then from the Contact tab, under the Communicate grouping, you select E-mail to open an e-mail message template with the e-mail address of the contact already included.

Another way to use the Address Book is when you are actually writing an e-mail message. If you select the To button or the CC button, it will bring you to a view of your contacts that will allow you to add people to the To, Cc and Bcc parts of your e-mail message, as shown in Figure 7.6. Another way to reach the Address Book for adding names to your message is by selecting the Address Book from the Names grouping off the Message ribbon.

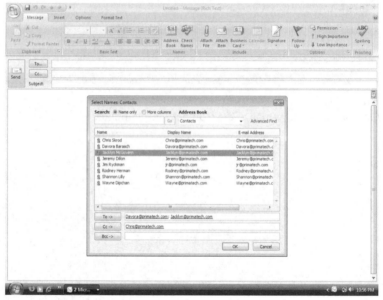

Figure 7.6
Using the Address Book to add contacts to your message.

Important

Before sending an e-mail you might want to check to ensure all the names included in the To, Cc or Bcc portions are correct. To do this, first complete the adding of e-mail addresses to your message (either manually, or through the Address Book) and then, from the **Message** ribbon, under the **Names** grouping, select the **Check Names** button.

→ Receiving E-mails

Typically, Outlook will retrieve e-mails for you when you start the application. If you have a permanent Internet connection, Outlook will connect to your e-mail servers to retrieve new mail according to the time settings configured under the Tools menu. Under Send/Receive, then Send/Receive Settings, select Send/Receive Groups (or select Ctrl+Alt+S). The default setting is 30 minutes.

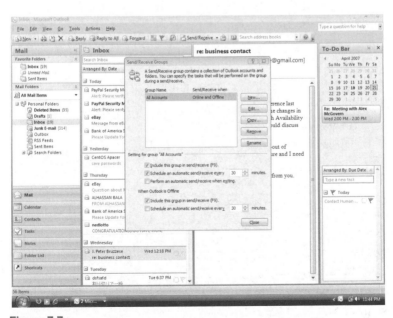

Figure 7.7
Changing the time frame for checking in with the mail servers.

Timesaver tip

You can force Outlook to check for new mail immediately by pressing the Send/Receive button located on the Standard toolbar. You can also press **F9** to force Outlook to check for new messages.

Notification Options

When you receive new e-mail you will typically receive a notification. This notification can be a sound, a change of the mouse cursor, an envelope icon in the notification area or a mail desktop alert (which will display a mini-message in the bottom right-hand corner of your screen).

To alter these settings you need to go to Tools, Options and under the Preferences tab, select E-mail Options. Then select Advanced E-mail Options. This will take you to the Advanced E-mail Options dialogue box, shown in Figure 7.8.

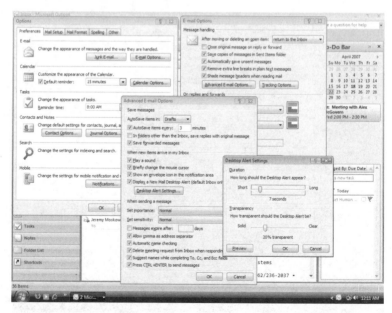

Figure 7.8
Altering your e-mail notification options.

From here you can turn certain notification options on and off. If you select the Desktop Alert Settings button it will take you to a dialogue that lets you establish the duration for the message (the default is 7 seconds) and the transparency setting (the default is 20%). You can select the Preview button to see how your notification will appear when you receive new mail.

Previewing Messages

Once your new mail is in your inbox, you obviously want to read it. Sometimes, though, you might be so busy that you don't want to read every word, but you want to quickly preview what you receive. The Reading Pane really helps increase your e-mail reading speed, which is great because "time is money".

Timesaver tip

You can preview the first three lines of messages in the main Outlook window by selecting the View menu and choosing AutoPreview. This will work along with the Reading Pane to increase your ability to determine whether you want to read an e-mail.

To preview a message in the Reading Pane, all you have to do is select the message and the contents will appear in the pane, as shown in Figure 7.9. You can quickly read a message and make a decision about whether you want to send a response, which you can do with one click of the Reply button.

Important

The Reading Pane can increase your productivity with Outlook, but it can also keep you safer from malicious scripts and/or attachments because you don't officially open the e-mail so nothing executes. Outlook 2007 has many safeguards in place already to protect you (and, if you are running Outlook 2007 on a Windows Vista system you are even more secure). However, the Reading Pane adds one more security layer.

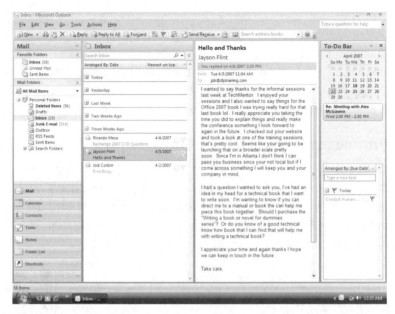

Figure 7.9
Working with the Reading Pane.

Navigating Messages with the Reading Pane

There are some suggestions in using the Reading Pane efficiently that you may want to consider. To begin with, from your main window for mail, select the Unread Mail folder (which should be located in your Favorites folders). To quickly move through your messages you can use the following shortcut keys:

■ Use the spacebar to scroll down through messages until you reach the bottom of a message. You also use the spacebar to move to the next message.

■ Hit Ctrl+R to reply to a message.

■ Hit Ctrl+Shift+R to reply to all.

■ Hit the Delete key to delete the message.

Previewing Attachments with the Reading Pane

Sometimes you receive an attachment and just want to quickly see what it contains. You can preview the file through the Reading Pane if it is supported. Files that are supported by default include Word 2007, Excel 2007, PowerPoint 2007, Visio 2007 drawings, images and text files.

Keep in mind that these messages can be previewed only if the sender used HTML or Plain Text as their messaging format. If they used Rich Text, you cannot preview the attachments.

To preview an attachment, perform the following:

1 From the message list, select your message with the attachment you wish to preview.

2 From the **Reading Pane**, select the attachment, as shown in Figure 7.10. The attachment will display itself in the Reading Pane. If it is a multiple-page document, or slideshow, you can use the slider navigation bar to move to other pages or slides.

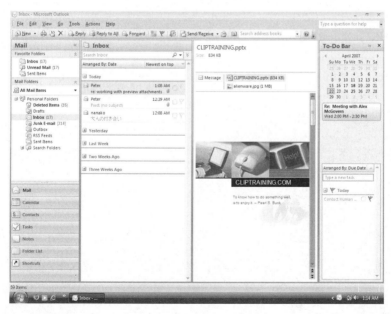

Figure 7.10
Using the Reading Pane to preview attachments.

8

Adding Visual Appeal to Your E-mails

In this lesson you'll learn about personalising your e-mails using stationery, themes, colours, graphics and signatures.

→ Using Stationery and Themes

Just because you are using e-mail doesn't mean you have to remove all personality from your messages. While many work-related e-mails are simply text, for those messages that you want to personalise a bit you can go a bit further and include some colour with stationery.

Keep in mind that you can change the font type, colour and size in any message you create. So, when we say "stationery" we are referring to the background of your e-mail, not the actual content.

Creating a Single Message with Stationery or Theme

Finding the way to create an e-mail that uses stationery might be frustrating at first because it isn't apparent. However, here is how it is done:

1 Go to the **Mail** navigation button first to ensure you have access to the actions associated with mail.

2 Now select the **Action** menu and scroll down to **New Mail Message Using**, then select **More Stationery**.

3 From the **Theme or Stationery** dialogue box, shown in Figure 8.1, select the stationery you prefer. You'll notice that an example of that stationery will appear in the "Sample of stationery" section.

4 Select **OK** and the new message will appear with the stationery you've selected, as shown in Figure 8.2.

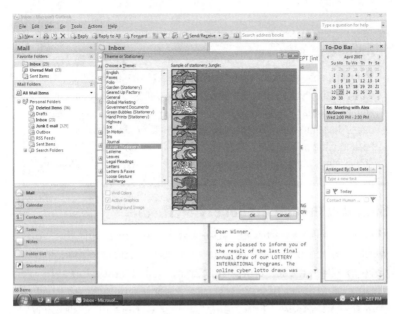

Figure 8.1
Using stationery to add personality to your e-mail.

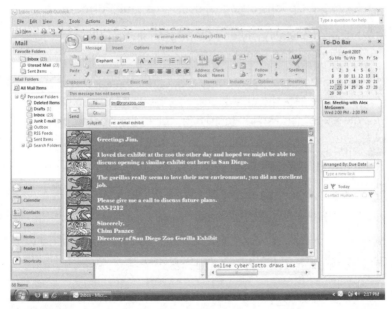

Figure 8.2
Stationery slides into the background of your message.

Important

You might note that some of the options in the Theme or Stationery dialogue go beyond stationery (which is your e-mail background) but actually offer to customise your e-mail in other ways, more like a web page. These are called Themes and they can alter not only the background but how text and bullets appear in your e-mail message. All of this is made possible if you are using HTML as your message format.

Setting a Default Stationery or Theme

Maybe you like a particular type of stationery or theme that you want to send out with all of your e-mails but you don't want to have to select it each time. You can actually change the settings in Outlook 2007 to have one stationery or theme applied to all your new messages. To accomplish this, perform the following:

1 Select the **Tools** menu, then select **Options**.

2 From the Options dialogue, select the **Mail Format** tab.

3 Notice the Stationery and Fonts grouping and select **Stationery and Fonts** button.

4 On the **Personal Stationery** tab, under the section at the top that says "Theme or stationery for new HTML e-mail message" (shown in Figure 8.3), select the **Theme** button.

5 Select the theme or stationery you prefer for newer messages and hit OK.

6 From the Signatures and Stationery dialogue hit OK and close out of the other boxes.

Now when you start new mail messages you will automatically be given the theme or stationery you selected.

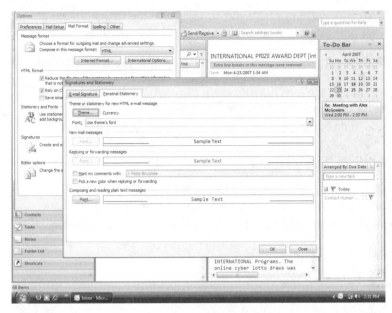

Figure 8.3
Setting a default theme or stationery.

Important

Once you have a theme or stationery established you can return to the same settings area and turn it off if you need to. However, you can also select the Actions menu and under New Mail Message Using, you can see that you have the option to use HTML (No Stationery) to compose an e-mail that will not use the stationery or theme you have selected.

→ Adding Colour and Graphics to Your Messages

There are several ways to spruce up your mail messages. One way is by using the Font tools to change the type, size and colour of your text (including bold, indent and underline). But there are two other ways in which you can improve the look and feel of your messages with a little colour and some graphics:

- By adding illustrations, which can include pictures, Clip Art, shapes, SmartArt or Excel charts.

- By changing the theme for your message. (Note: This theme setting is different from the ones we discussed earlier.)

Adding Illustrations

As with any document, you may want to add a picture or some other type of graphic element to your e-mail to make it more interesting, or informative. To do this, perform the following:

1 Begin a new e-mail.

2 Select the **Insert** tab.

3 From the Illustrations grouping, note the options you have, as shown in Figure 8.4. These include the following:

   a Pictures: You can add pictures of almost any standard type, including .bmp, jpg, gif, png, tif and more.

   b Clip Art: Allows you to insert images that have been created for you to use (free of charge) from Microsoft.

   c Shapes: You can insert shapes as simple as a line, or as complicated as a starburst that you can add text into.

   d SmartArt: Is a fancy way to display flow charts and organisation charts, as shown in Figure 8.4.

   e Chart: Enables you to create Excel charts that are placed directly within your e-mail message.

4 Select the type of Illustration you wish to add, then either locate it in your personal system (as with pictures and/or Clip Art) or find it in Microsoft's Clip Art gallery, or draw it yourself.

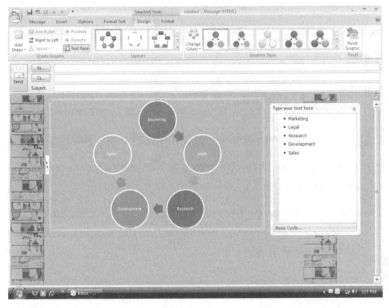

Figure 8.4
Working with a SmartArt diagram.

Themes

Other aspects of an e-mail message are the Theme settings and Page Color options. These can be found within a message template, from the Options ribbon, under the Themes grouping.

A theme is a preconfigured selection of colours, fonts and effects settings. There are 20 preconfigured themes that come with Word, Excel, PowerPoint and Outlook. These allow you to select a theme to develop consistency between all your applications. This cultivates a look that says "uniformity" to clients because all of the fonts and colours will match between your documentation (and e-mail) and any shapes or SmartArt you add to your message will match (that is, will have the same formatting appearance and colour) those shapes and SmartArt diagrams you have in your documentation.

You can create specialised themes if you like. If you create a personal theme in one application (Word, Excel, PowerPoint or Outook), that theme will be available in all the other applications so that you need to create the theme only once.

To select a theme for your e-mail message, perform the following:

1 From within your message template, select the **Options** ribbon.

2 From within the Themes grouping, select the **Themes** button and note the 20 preconfigured themes, as shown in Figure 8.5.

3 From the Themes options, select one of the following:

a   Reset to Theme from Template: To reset your message to the default.

b   More Themes on Microsoft Office Online: To search through the Microsoft site for additional themes, as they become available.

c   Browse for Themes: To search for themes that you have saved in the past that you want to apply.

d   Save Current Theme: If you have done some configuration changes through the Colors, Fonts and Effects options (which are also conveniently located on the Themes grouping), you can save the selection as a theme template for future use.

Page Color is another option from the Themes grouping that will allow you to alter the background of the page. Now, you will recall with using stationery that it doesn't affect the actual content of the page, but it will alter the appearance of your e-mail.

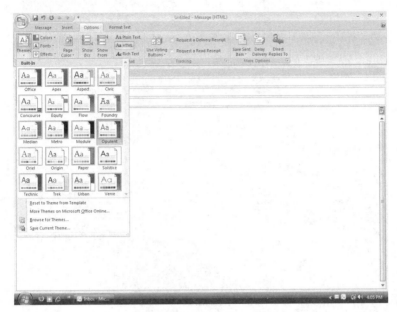

Figure 8.5
Choosing from among the 20 preconfigured themes.

If you select this Page Color option you can quickly choose a new colour for your page (keep in mind that if you choose a new colour, you may also need to change the font colour to something lighter so that it will show up against the darker background). If, however, you select Fill Effects, you will be taken to the Fill Effects dialogue box where you will be presented with four options, as shown in Figure 8.6:

■ Gradient: Allows you to determine colour choices for the background (or you can select from a preset colour array).

■ Texture: Allows you to choose from a predesigned pattern, such as Marble, Granite, Sand, Water droplets and so forth.

■ Pattern: Allows you to determine a colourful pattern to your background that looks like blocks, or lines, or dots and uses whichever colours you prefer.

■ Picture: Allows you to use a picture as your background.

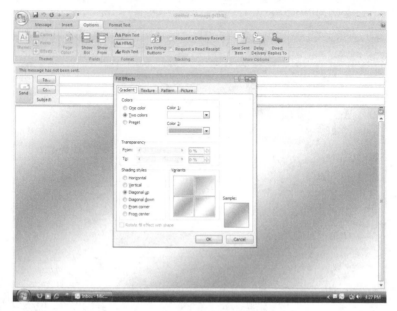

Figure 8.6
Changing your page colour.

Timesaver tip

Using some of these techniques to create impressive e-mails can be very helpful. For example, you can create an e-mail invitation to a baby shower, using a picture of a baby as a watermark in the background. Your options are limitless.

→ Using E-mail Signatures

In Outlook you can create a signature to be attached at the end of your e-mail. This signature can be as simple as a short block of unformatted text, or as complicated as an entire business card, with your picture attached.

You can even create more than one signature – perhaps one for business correspondence and one for your personal e-mail. These signatures can be added to or removed from e-mails at your choosing.

Creating an E-mail Signature

To create an e-mail signature, perform the following:

1 From your main Outlook window, select **Tools** and then **Options**.

2 Select the **Mail Format** tab.

3 Select the **Signatures** button. The E-mail Signature tab shows you all the signatures you have created.

4 Select the **New** option and give your signature a name.

5 In the **Edit Signature** dialogue, you can enter the text you want for your signature and format that text using the formatting toolbar, as shown in Figure 8.7.

6 You can select the **Picture** button to add a picture to your signature. (Note: If the picture is too large, you will have to use an editing tool to shrink it. The signature tool doesn't provide a way for you to crop or shrink your images.) Another option is for you to select the Business Card button to easily add an entire business card (with address, picture and so forth included).

7 Select the hyperlink button if you want to create a link to your website within your signature.

8 When you have completed your signature, select the Save option. Now you can create additional signatures, or click OK to close the dialogue.

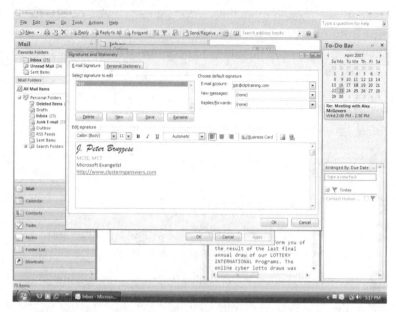

Figure 8.7
Creating a signature for your e-mail.

Timesaver tip

If you want to use a signature when you create a new message or when you reply to messages that you have received, adjust the settings in the Choose Default Signature to use the signature you have just created.

Important

To create a business card that you can use for your signatures, you can use the Contacts application. Your card can include all of your contact information and a picture and you can select this card from Contacts when you select the Business Card button from the E-mail Signature dialogue box. One important thing to note is that the two are not linked, so if you update information on your business card, it will not update in the signature. You will have to edit your signature and reselect the card that has been edited.

Edit or Delete an E-mail Signature

You can edit any of your signatures by returning to the E-mail Signature dialogue and selecting the signature you wish to edit from the "Select signature to edit" dialogue.

The signature will show up in the "Edit signature" window and you can make any changes you like. Just remember to save the changes when you have finished.

In addition, you can select a signature and click **Delete** to remove it from your list of usable signatures.

How to Use a Signature

Typically, when you create a signature, you select the option to have that signature included in new messages you create and in messages that you reply to others with. If that is the case, you will automatically see your signature whenever you select the New mail message option. It will be located within your message template.

If, however, you do not have the message automatically included, you can do the following to insert the signature:

1 From within your message template, select the **Insert** ribbon.

2 From the Include grouping, select the **Signature** button.

3 Select the signature and it will be added to your message. Note: If you have more than one signature, you can choose to switch between them when you create a message.

4 If you have edits to make on a signature, you can also select the Signatures option and it will return you to the E-mail Signature tab.

Timesaver tip

Even if you have a default signature established for your messages, you can quickly change between signatures by using the Signature options located on the Insert ribbon under the Include grouping.

→ Equations, Symbols and Horizontal Lines

There are times when you may need to include within your e-mail certain equations or symbols. These equations might be something as simple as E=mc2, or as complicated as $\frac{-b \pm \sqrt{b^2-4ac}}{2a}$. Symbols can include ™, or ©, or even mathematical symbols. Horizontal lines can be used to divide up your message into groupings.

While in your message template, to use equations, symbols, or horizontal lines, go to the Insert ribbon, under the Symbols grouping, where you will see the three options to work with these graphical features.

9

Working with E-mail Options

In this lesson you'll be introduced to e-mail options including message, security and delivery settings.

→ What Are E-mail Options?

With normal e-mail applications, you complete your e-mail and hit Send and that is the end of your options. It's true that even well-experienced Outlook users believe that e-mail is limited in areas like confirmation of receipt, controlled delivery times and issues of this type.

In actuality, Outlook 2007 has several features that can really be beneficial, especially for business users and people who work within a larger company.

To see the options available to you, begin a new e-mail message. From within the message template, select the Options ribbon and notice the Tracking and More Options groupings. You can use these settings to add special settings to your message before sending it. You can also select the little dialogue box launcher in the corner of the groupings to reveal the Message Options dialogue, shown in Figure 9.1.

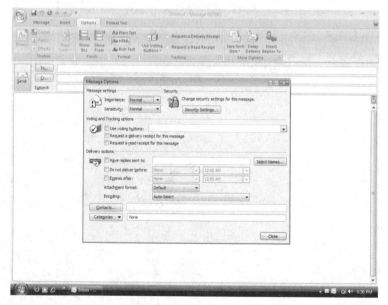

Figure 9.1
Working with Message Options.

There is a connection between the options on the ribbon and the options within the dialogue box and you can use either one to perform the tasks you need, although the dialogue contains even more settings and options.

Important

Most of these options require that the recipients are using Outlook as their e-mail application and, as is the case with the Voting options, some of these options require that both the sender and the recipient are using exchange servers.

Message Settings

Your message settings allow you to configure the importance level of your message and the sensitivity level. Establishing these settings can indicate to a recipient whether they need to respond quickly to a message or whether it can be put off until a later time.

■ Importance levels can be Low, Normal or High. Users will see a blue down arrow for Low and a red exclamation point for High.

■ Sensitivity levels can be Normal, Personal, Private or Confidential. This setting will be displayed in the message header for the document so the recipient can see it clearly.

Timesaver tip

You can quickly select importance levels for a message by going to the Message ribbon. Under the Options grouping you can select the **High or Low** buttons.

Security Settings

These settings allow you to encrypt the contents and attachments of your e-mail, or add a digital signature and/or certificate to ensure higher levels of security for your message. The wide scope of these settings is beyond the range of this book; however, the Outlook Help files can assist in establishing stronger levels of security for your Outlook messages.

To perform the task of encrypting or digitally signing your messages, you need to be given a Digital ID from either an external certificate authority (for Internet e-mail) or from your exchange server administrator (for internal e-mail).

Jargon buster

Encrypting a message makes it unreadable by anyone other than its intended recipient. The way this works is that the message is converted into ciphered text. This means it is jumbled. Only the person who has the proper key can open it or decipher the message.

A **digital signature** is a way for you to provide proof to the recipient that you are who you say you are. You obtain a certificate from a third party who verifies your identity and you use that certificate to "sign", in a sense, your message. The recipient can check your certificate against the third-party provided to ensure that you are not an imposter.

Voting Options

At times you may need responses from individuals within your company. You can send a message that requests the recipient chooses the following:

■ Approve, Reject

■ Yes, No

■ Yes, No, Maybe.

Now, these options can be selected quickly for a message from the Options ribbon, under the Tracking grouping. You select the Use Voting Buttons option and then select the type of vote you want. Note: You can also select the options from the Message Options dialogue.

When the recipient receives an e-mail that includes the request for a vote, that request will be in the message header. If you are reading the message from the Reading Pane, the message will say "Click here to vote". The recipient selects the link and voting options and will be presented with the message shown in Figure 9.2. If, however, you have opened the message, you can vote by selecting your choice from the Message ribbon, under the Respond grouping, by selecting Vote and your option. Then you will be presented with the message in Figure 9.2.

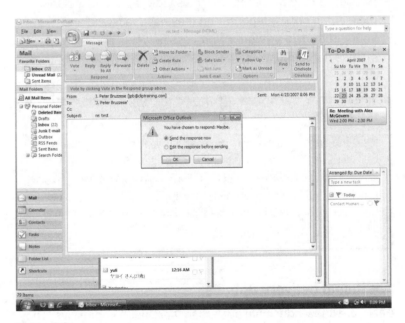

Figure 9.2
Voting options.

You can choose "Send the response now" or "Edit the response before sending", which allows you to add text to the message being sent. Once the response has been sent, you can keep track of your responses by returning to the message. Now, in the message header, it will tell you what you voted.

Delivery and/or Read Receipts

There are two checkboxes located on the Options ribbon, under the Tracking grouping. They are:

■ Request a delivery receipt for this message: This is a message that is sent back to the sender when the message is delivered to the recipient's mailbox. But there is no indication that the recipient has read your e-mail.

■ Request a read receipt for this message: This requests the recipient to send a reply saying they have received and read your e-mail. It is a voluntary process however and many people choose not to reply.

Important

If you use these options within your company you will see them work well. However, if you are using them over the Internet you will most likely receive a message back from an SMTP server saying that delivery receipts are not supported. You will still be able to receive the Read receipt, but it will be up to the recipient as to whether or not they wish to send the receipt.

Additional Delivery Options

There are a few additional options that are quite impressive. They include the following:

■ Direct Replies To: This button, located on the Options ribbon off the More Options grouping, is useful when you send out a message for which you wish to have replies given to a different account. So, a person receives the e-mail and hits Reply. In the To bar, instead of your address being listed, the address of the person you have configured as the redirected recipient will be in the bar.

■ Delay Delivery: This option allows you to compose a message and send it, but it will not be "sent" literally until the date you provide. It will just sit in your outbox. This is an excellent option when you need to have an e-mail sent on a certain day or at a particular time of day but you know you will not be available to send it. You can establish delayed delivery. In order for this to work you have to have Outlook (and your computer, of course) up and running. You also may want to alter the settings for your Send/Receive Mail options to automatically send and receive mail on a timelier basis.

Important

With Delayed Delivery, if you try to close Outlook you will be given a warning message that there are still items in your outbox. That isn't a problem if you know you will be returning and restarting Outlook at a time before your system is configured to send the e-mail. But it's a good warning so you don't forget that your delayed mail will not be sent if Outlook is off (or your system is shut down).

■ Expires After: This is one setting that isn't on the ribbon (like the other two) but can be found only from within the Message Options dialogue box. The purpose of this setting is to send messages that have expiration times on them. For example, let's say you have a meeting invitation going out to people in your department. The meeting is at 1pm and you want to send out a reminder. You can set the message to expire at 1pm. What this will mean is, all those who didn't check their mail and didn't receive the message will not receive it. The exchange server will delete the message once the time has expired because the recipient didn't check their mail prior to the expiration time.

→ E-mail Options

In addition to configuring options for individual messages as they go out, you can establish settings for your e-mail process in general. You can configure how messages are handled and how replies and forwards are handled too.

To configure these options, from the main window select **Tools** and then **Options**. Select the **Preferences** tab and then the **E-mail Options** button. You will be taken to the E-mail Options dialogue (as shown in Figure 9.3), which will offer you two groupings of options: "Message handling" and "On replies and forwards".

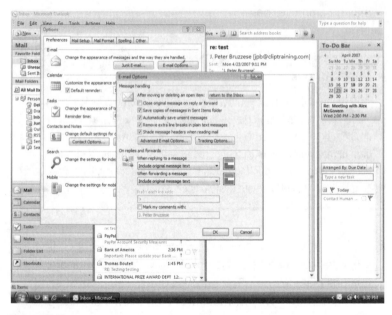

Figure 9.3
E-mail Options.

Under the "Message Handling" section, you are offered some intuitive choices for how you want your e-mail to function. For example, you can choose the "Save copies of messages in Sent

Items folder", which will save a copy of every message you sent so you can reference back later.

If you select the Tracking Options button, you will be taken to the Tracking Options dialogue, shown in Figure 9.4. From here you can configure all messages you send to request Read or Delivery receipts. Usually this is not recommended. It's best to request these only when you really want them. You can also establish automatically how you want your system to handle Read receipts. You can tell it to send a reply always, never or "Ask me before sending a response".

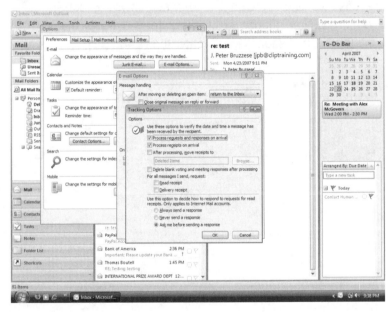

Figure 9.4
Tracking Options dialogue.

The section in the E-mail Options dialogue called "On replies and forwards" allows you to configure how you want reply and forward e-mails to be handled. For example, have you ever noticed that some people reply to you and your message is included in the reply? Some even have your message clearly highlighted with a >

character as a prefix before each line of the message you sent. This is all accomplished through these settings.

Here are your options for reply and forwarded e-mails:

■ Do not include original message.

■ Attach original message (which will send along your message as an attachment that the recipient can open if they wish).

■ Include original message text.

■ Include and indent original message text.

■ Prefix each line of the original message. (If you select this option you can choose which character is used for the prefix, although the default is the "greater than" sign (>).)

10

Managing E-mail

In this lesson you'll learn how to manage your e-mail using message flags and rules. You'll also learn how to search for items in Outlook 2007.

→ Using Categories

Outlook is more than a business tool (although it is more commonly seen in corporate environments) – it is a tool to help us communicate with friends and family, and a tool that helps us balance and organise our many responsibilities. One of the ways it does this is by helping us easily organise our affairs through the use of categories that are structured by colours. You can assign a category to e-mail, contacts, appointments, meetings and tasks.

To see a list of categories and rename them to personal settings, select the **Action** menu and then **Categorize**. Select the **All Categories** option to see a listing of all the categories and their colours. You can add new categories, modify the colours or names of existing categories, or delete a category.

You can assign more than one category to an item, which can be very helpful. The colourful icon will show up to three different categories for an item, although you can assign more than three. The categories will show up in the message header as well.

Timesaver tip

You can use the quick click method of assigning a category to your message, by selecting the little category icon. With this option you can quick-click only one pre-chosen colour. You can, however, right-click the icon and choose a different colour or apply multiple categories.

→ Flagging Messages for Follow-up

You can apply a flag to a message (or contact) to give you a reminder that you need to follow up with a specific item or person. There are default flags that have dates already chosen for you, although you can customise these for whichever dates you need.

There are several ways to add a flag to a message. One way is from within the message itself. If you open your message and look on the **Message** ribbon, there is a grouping called **Options**. You can select the **Follow Up** button and choose one of the pre-selected times (shown in Figure 10.1), or choose a custom time that you can configure (shown in Figure 10.2).

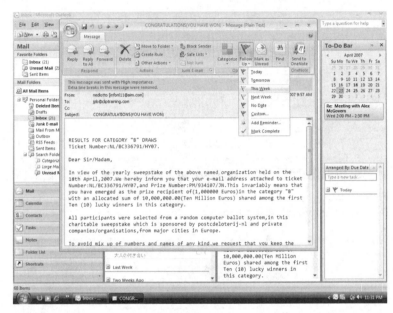

Figure 10.1
Choosing one of the default follow-up flags.

Notice that you can also set a reminder that will play a sound if you like. To change to a different sound, select the little sound icon and browse to a different sound file.

Adding a Quick-Click Flag

You can add a flag to a message easily by using the Flag Status column from the main window. If you right-click on the flag, you can quickly establish a follow-up (as shown in Figure 10.3). If you just select the flag (hence the name "quick-click flag") you will set a follow-up for Today (which is the default setting).

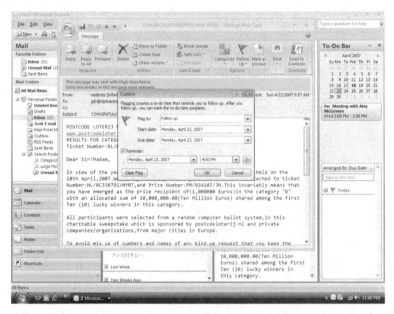

Figure 10.2

Setting a custom follow-up flag.

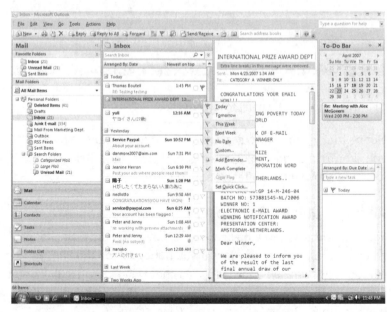

Figure 10.3

Working with the Quick-Click flag.

Timesaver tip

Too many times people forget to follow up on that one e-mail of the day that they thought they would get back to. Using quick-click flags is the easiest way to give yourself a reminder of the activities you need to follow up on for that day.

Send a Message Flag to Others

You may need to help some of the people you e-mail to respond to you. I have one friend and co-worker who I know is in the office and at his desk each day, yet somehow he seems to have difficulty remembering to e-mail me back. Adding a flag to his messages is just the thing to help jog his memory a bit.

To add a follow-up flag to an e-mail you send, perform the following:

1 Begin a new message and fill in the details and content of the message.

2 On the **Message** ribbon, under the **Options** grouping, select the **Follow Up** button.

3 Select the **Flag for Recipients** option and a Custom dialogue box will appear with options for you to set a message for yourself and for recipients, as shown in Figure 10.4.

4 You can select the checkbox **Flag for Me** which will allow you to remind yourself of something in harmony with this message.

5 In the **Flag to** option you can select one of the following options: Call, Do Not Forward, Follow Up, For Your Information, Forward, No Response Necessary, Read, Reply, Reply to All and Review.

6 You can even provide them with a reminder (although you cannot establish the sound that will play).

7 Once complete, select **OK** and then **Send** the message.

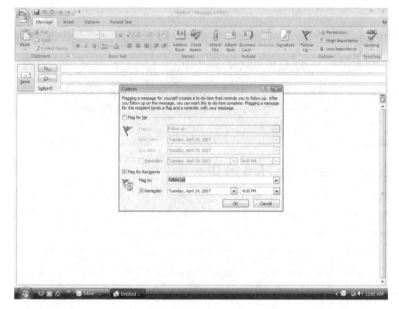

Figure 10.4
Setting a flag for recipients.

Completing a Follow-up

Your Outlook cannot know whether you followed up in the way you were supposed to. You have to tell it that the item is completed. You can do this by clearing the flag from the item, but this will remove any record of the follow-up.

Rather than remove the flag, you could mark the follow-up as complete. To do this you can select the item in your main window and change the flag to a checkmark. Or, from within the message, you can select the **Follow Up** button, located on the **Message** ribbon under the **Options** grouping, and select "Mark Complete". The date the item was marked complete will be displayed in the InfoBar.

→ Creating Message Folders

Ten e-mails per day over the course of one year is 3,500 e-mails. That is just one year! While some of that is junk mail you can remove and some you will just delete once you've read it, the fact is you will still be faced with a tremendous amount of mail to organise. Now, you can always use the search features to find an e-mail from the past, but another great way to handle all that mail is through the use of new folders.

To create a new mail message folder, perform the following:

1 Select the **File** menu and then hover your mouse over **New**.

2 Select **Folder** and the "Create a New Folder" dialogue will appear, as shown in Figure 10.5. Note: You could also right-click one of the root folders (such as the Inbox) and select **New Folder** to reach the same dialogue.

3 Provide a name for the folder. Ensure that the folder contains "Mail and Post Items" and then select the location of the new folder.

4 When you have finished, select OK. Your new folder is ready to receive mail.

5 Now you can either drag your mail into the new folder for organising or you can create a mail rule that will move new mail that meets the rules specifications into that folder.

Where to Place Your New Folders

Location, location, location! You can place these folders at the root of your folder structure so that they reside in the same location as the Inbox. You could create a single folder called "Organising Mail" (or something of your choosing) and place sub-folders within that folder. Or you could just nest these folders within your Inbox (or any of the other root folders). The choice is really up to you. You need to determine what location is going to be the most productive for you.

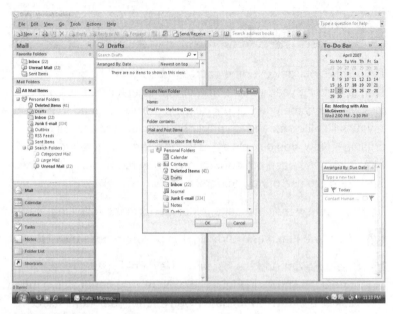

Figure 10.5
Working with Message Options.

→ Using Search Folders

Moving your e-mail messages into folders you create can help you tremendously when it's time to search for an e-mail. There are various ways to search for specific e-mails. One way is through search folders. These aren't really folders that we create like we did in the last section, they are virtual folders. In other words, they look like a normal folder, but in actuality the contents of these folders may reside in different locations – they appear in the search folder only because they come under specific search criteria.

A good example of a search folder is the "Unread" folder in Outlook. When you select this folder, it can pull messages from many different folders into this one folder because it knows you want to see all unread messages. That is the criterion and so the search folder dynamically updates itself.

The concept may be difficult to understand at first, but once you create a few folders it will start to come together. So for starters let's create a new search folder. To do this, perform the following:

1 From your Navigation pane, right-click the **Search Folders** section and choose **New Search Folder**.

2 The New Search Folder dialogue will appear, as shown in Figure 10.6.

3 Select one of the preconfigured Search Folder criteria. In some cases, like "Unread Mail", no further input is required and you can select OK. In other cases you have to specify more detail. For example, if you select the option "Mail from specific people" you then have to choose the people you are referring to.

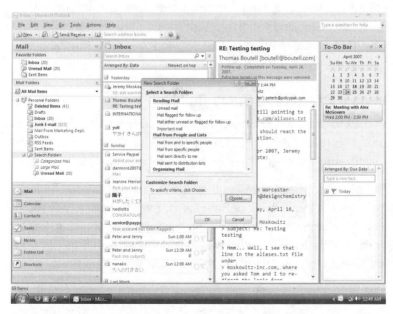

Figure 10.6
Creating search folders.

→ Searching for Items in Outlook 2007

Search folders are very helpful in getting a pool of search results, not necessarily for finding that one e-mail message we are looking for. If we are looking for all the messages that have attachments over 1MB in size, a search folder will work perfectly. But there are two other ways to search for items more conveniently.

Instant Search and Query Builder

At the top of every Outlook folder view there is an Instant Search box. This search box will look through messages and attachments to find what you are looking for in a matter of seconds.

To use Instant Search, select the folder you need to search (this includes the Inbox itself, or Sent items, basically any folder you wish to search through). Select the Instant Search box and begin typing. Immediately, Outlook will try to locate the message(s) you are looking for, displaying results for searches as you type.

If you need to expand your search, or you have a complicated search, you might want to use the Query Builder, shown in Figure 10.7. While Instant Search is great if you are looking for specific names or words, the Query Builder lets you specify multiple search criteria. For example, you need to find all the e-mails sent by your manager from 10 October to 30 June with the subject "Special Project". To view the Query Builder you can select the double down arrow next to the Instant Search box (or you can select the Tools menu, then Instant Search and then Expand the Query Builder).

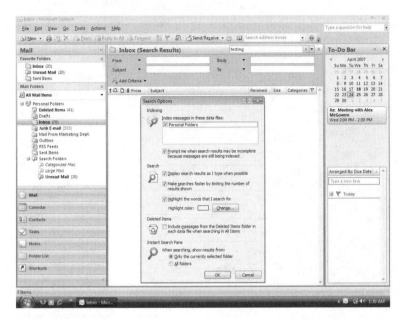

Figure 10.7
The Query Builder.

If you want to make any changes to the way your search options are configured, you can select Tools, Instant Search and then Instant Search Options, also shown in Figure 10.7.

From within these options you can configure certain indexing and search settings. You can decide whether you want Deleted Items searched as well, or how you want the Instant Search to work.

Advanced Find

Going one step further in terms of search ability is the Advanced Find tool. Even beyond the Query Builder, the Advanced Find tool can really narrow down your search criteria.

To use Advanced Find, choose Tools, Instant Search, then Advanced Find (or you can simply type Ctrl+Shift+F). The dialogue, shown in Figure 10.8, will reveal several tabs (Messages, More Choices and Advanced) to help you refine your search.

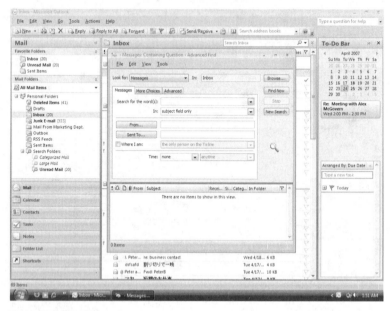

Figure 10.8
Using Advanced Find.

As we mentioned above, you can use the Advanced Find tool to establish an incredible level of criteria for your search and you can go one step further in that you can save the search criteria into a search folder.

To do this, perform the following:

1 First, define your search criteria until you are confident that this is the exact configuration you want for a search folder.

2 Select the **File** option from Advanced Find.

3 Select **Save Search as Search Folder**.

4 Give the folder a name and hit OK.

→ Working with Outlook Rules

Rules within Outlook has been, and continues to be, a very powerful tool. When you establish a rule, Outlook will examine messages as they come in (or go out, depending on the kind of rule) and will determine whether they meet the criteria of the rule and then perform a prescribed action.

Create a Rule

There are two types of rules really, simplistic and advanced. Now there is something to be said for simplicity, because sometimes that is all you are looking for from a rule. Let's say, for example, that all you want is for an e-mail message from a specific person to go into a folder you've created for that person. Simple enough.

To accomplish this task, the easy way to create that rule is to find a message from the person you wish to have rerouted, right-click on the message from the message list and select Create Rule. The Create Rule dialogue, shown in Figure 10.9, will appear.

10

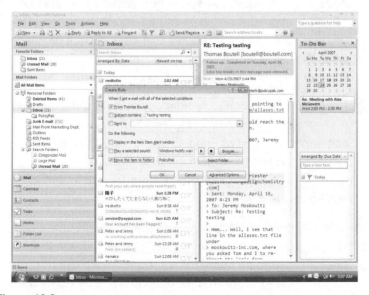

Figure 10.9
Creating a Basic Rule.

From within the Create Rule dialogue you can easily select from several common options, including establishing rules for sounds to be played when mail comes from that individual, or moving their mail to a specific folder, etc.

If, however, you want to make more advanced style rules, you can select the Advanced Options button. Note: You can also create advanced rules from scratch by selecting the Tools, Rules and Alerts option, which will bring you into a special dialogue for the creation, modification and removal of rules.

To create a rule from scratch, perform the following:

1 From within your **Outlook** main menu, select the **Tools** menu, then **Rules and Alerts**.

2 Within the **Rules and Alerts** dialogue, from the E-mail Rules tab, select **New**.

3 From the Rules Wizard's initial screen you have to decide whether you want to choose a template to follow for your rule. (This basically gives you a starting point for your rule – items such as "Move messages from someone to a folder" or "Delete a conversation" exist in the templates section.) Or you can select a blank template that says "Check messages when they arrive" or "Check messages after sending". Choose your option and select **Next**.

4 Now you need to configure your condition and the criteria for that condition, as shown in Figure 10.10. For example, you can select "marked as importance" for your condition. But then you still need to determine which level of importance (Low, Normal, High) to look for. Determine your conditions and select Next.

5 Now you need to configure the action you want taken. Do you want the message that meets the conditions in the previous step to be moved to a specific folder, deleted, forwarded, and so forth? Your options are extensive. Define your actions and select **Next**.

6 Now you can configure exceptions to the rule. Here you can establish whether there are ever times when a rule doesn't apply. Determine your exceptions and hit **Next**.

7 The final step involves providing a name and determining whether you want the rule to be applied to messages that already exist in the Inbox. You can examine the rule once more to make sure the settings are correct and then select **Finish**.

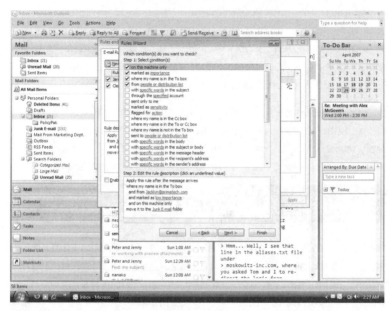

Figure 10.10
Configuring your rule conditions.

Out-of-Office Replies

When you are out of the office and want people to receive an e-mail back from you to indicate that you are out and possibly provide some details regarding how long you expect to be away, there are several ways to accomplish this depending on the type of e-mail account you have configured to use Outlook 2007.

For example, if you are using Outlook with an exchange server, you will actually see a tool called the "Out of Office Assistant" from the Tools menu. This tool can be configured to perform quite a number of tasks and if used with Exchange 2007 (the latest e-mail server), the functionality is even better than ever.

If you are using a standard Internet POP3 e-mail account, you can still have an out-of-office response provided by your system; you will just need to use the rules that we discussed earlier to accomplish this. First you will create a message template with your out-of-office reply message and then you will need to configure a rule that responds to all e-mails coming in using that template e-mail. Keep in mind that for this to work, your system has to be up and running and so does Outlook.

For more details on the Out of Office Assistant and/or how to create automated replies, see the help file article "Automatically reply to incoming messages while out of the office".

→ Fight Spam with Junk E-mail Filters

I set up a new e-mail account exactly one month ago. I am now the proud recipient of 21 Inbox messages and 333 junk mail spam messages. Incredible. As frustrated as I am about the spam, I would be even more frustrated if I didn't have an integrated spam filter. Sometimes within companies there is a spam filter on the e-mail server that will help mitigate the amount of spam you receive. In addition, however, it's always good to have a final wall between you and spam – your junk mail filter.

The junk mail filter is preconfigured, but you can tweak its settings over time to make sure junk mail is removed and good mail doesn't get accidentally included in with the junk.

To start with, you can open up the Junk E-mail Options by selecting the Actions menu, then Junk E-mail, then Junk E-mail Options. This will take you to the Junk E-mail Options dialogue, shown in Figure 10.11.

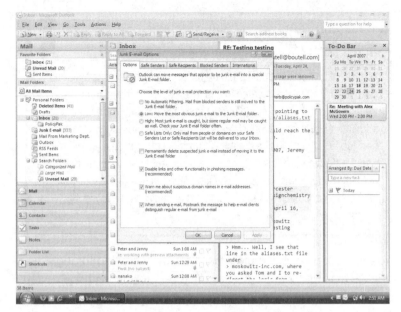

Figure 10.11
Working with junk e-mail options.

Your default setting for junk e-mail is Low. This will capture the most obvious junk e-mail and move it to the Junk E-mail folder. You can change this to High (although be careful, it may also grab quite a number of legitimate e-mails, so you have to scan your junk e-mail from time to time). You can also turn the junk filter off (although this isn't recommended). Or you can select "Safe Lists Only". If this is selected, only people in the Safe Senders list and Safe Recipients list will be delivered.

In addition, there is a Blocked Senders tab where you can stop any mail coming from a particularly offensive spammer. There is an International tab where you can block specific domains and/or encodings that you feel may be causing you difficulty with junk mail.

Important

One checkbox on the Options tab of the Junk E-mail Options dialogue disables links that are located in supposed phishing messages. It's important for your security that you leave this option selected. In addition, there is an option to permanently delete messages that are considered junk mail. The default is that this option is deselected. It's important to leave it this way because from time to time (quite often actually) a legitimate message will get placed in junk mail. You wouldn't want to permanently delete a real message, so leave this setting off.

You can educate your junk e-mail filter by searching through the Junk E-mail folder and when you find e-mail that isn't spam, don't move it but rather right-click the message and navigate to Junk E-mail, then select "Mark as Not Junk". This will move the message back into your Inbox and you will be asked whether you want to always trust that person in the future.

In addition, if you are receiving lots of junk e-mail in your Inbox, you can right-click the message, navigate to Junk E-mail and select one of the actions you wish to take with the spam, as shown in Figure 10.12. You can add a spammer to your list of blocked senders with a single click of the mouse.

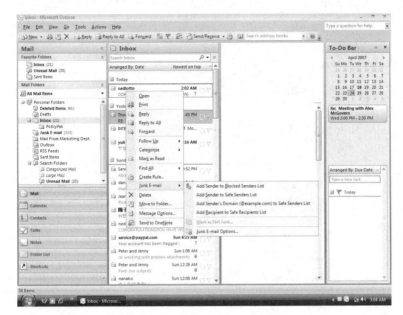

Figure 10.12
Educating your spam filter.

11

Using the Outlook Calendar

In this lesson you'll learn all about calendar options including how to customise your calendar, create appointments and work with meeting requests.

→ Navigating the Calendar

The integration of the calendar in Outlook is one of the highlights of the program. With the Outlook Calendar you are able to keep track of all your appointments and meetings, both business and personal. You can print the calendar, synchronise it with a Mobile PC or SmartPhone, or send your calendar to someone else for viewing.

First, you will need to learn how to work with the calendar and then in Chapter 12 we will show you how to use your calendar to collaborate with others.

When you first open the calendar you will quickly see that you have a calendar control (a mini calendar) called the Date Navigator above your Navigation pane. In the main window you have the option to switch your calendar views between Day, Week and Month (as you can see in Figure 11.1).

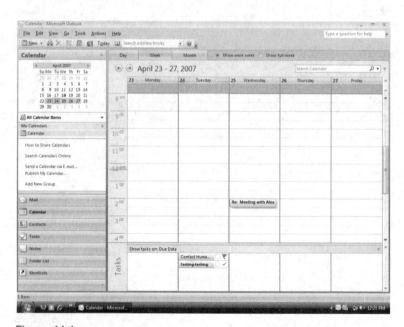

Figure 11.1
The default calendar view.

Timesaver tip

You can also have the To-Do present when you are working in the Calendar. To do this, select the View menu, then To-Do Bar. You can have it displayed normally or minimised. This will give you access to more tools at one time. If you find it gets in your way, use the minimised version to keep it hidden. Notice that your Date Navigator will switch sides to the To-Do Bar when it is enabled.

You can select any date in the Date Navigator and it will take you to that day, week, or month (depending on the view you have selected) for you to view appointments for the day.

It's easy to see which days you have scheduled appointments on because they are bold in the Date Navigator.

Timesaver tip

To move to other months, use the Date Navigator and select the arrows to the right or left to show you appointments both past and present. A quick way to go to the calendar month is to select the month itself. You will be shown three months before and three months after the current month.

11

Here are a few tips and tricks to manoeuvring around the calendar to make you more productive:

■ The Day view allows you to see all the tasks at hand for that day. If you are moving around your calendar and are on another date, you can select the Today button on the Standard toolbar to bring you back to the current day.

■ If you select the Week view, you can select one of the radio buttons "Show work week" in order to see only activity from Monday to Friday. This cuts out the weekends, which are typically used for non-business activities.

■ If you are in the Month view, you can quickly move to other months by using the right and left buttons at the top. You can also use the Page Up and Page Down buttons to navigate through the months.

Timesaver tip

To quickly move from the date you are on (in either Day, Week or Month views) to that same date one month ahead or behind, you can select Alt+Page Up, or Alt+Page Down.

→ Customising Your Calendar

If you want to make any changes to the way your calendar displays itself, you can start by making changes in its appearance. To do this, from any of the views (Day, Week, Month), right-click in a portion of empty space and select "Other Settings". This will bring up the Format Day/Week/Month View dialogue, as shown in Figure 11.2.

You can change the default font used to display items in your calendar and a few other settings. One setting that you may find useful is the ability to alter the time scale from its default of 30 minutes. This may be very helpful to people who bill their time in increments of 15 minutes. Or you can increase the time to 60 minutes to see more of your schedule at a glance.

Calendar Options

Another location for Calendar options can be found under the Tools menu, Options. From the Preferences tab you select Calendar Options and you will be taken to the dialogue shown in Figure 11.3.

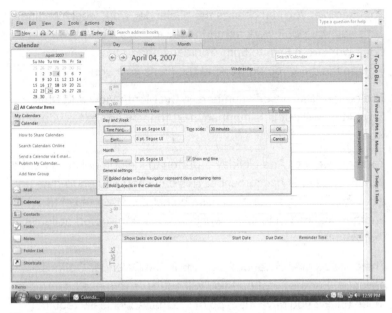

Figure 11.2
Changing some of the settings for your Day/Week/Month view.

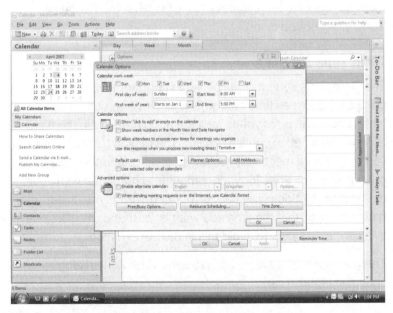

Figure 11.3
Making changes to your Calendar Options.

For example, you can change the "Calendar work week" settings. Let's say you don't work from Monday to Friday, or maybe you don't work from 8am to 5pm. You can change these days to include the days you do work, at the times you work.

The option "Show week numbers in the Month View and Date Navigator" will put little numbers next to the week to tell you what week of the year you are in.

You can use the "Add Holidays" button to include holidays from a variety of cultural backgrounds. This can keep you up to date on all of your holidays, but it can also be helpful if you travel to another destination to know what days are considered holidays in that country.

There are several advanced settings in the Calendar Options dialogue. For the most part you will not have to make changes to these unless you have the type of job that specifically requires you to publish your calendar for others to see (which is what the Free/Busy Options button assists you with) or if you handle meeting requests for resources (which is what the Resource Scheduling button is for).

Time Zone Settings

The Time Zone settings may be very important to you if you travel quite a bit between time zones. One aspect that can be helpful when you travel is for you to indicate appointments in the time zone of the location you are visiting. The reason for this is that you may miss a meeting if you schedule it for one time and then change the time zone for your computer to match up with your destination. Outlook will change your appointed time unless you have indicated that the time you want is for that particular zone. We will discuss how to avoid this in the next section.

There are several ways you can use the Time Zone dialogue, shown in Figure 11.4.

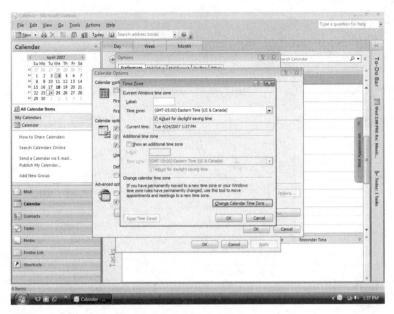

Figure 11.4
Working with the Time Zone dialogue box.

For starters, you can select the "Show an additional time zone". Establish the settings for your second zone and give both your home and away zones a heading, so you can easily see which one is which time, as shown in Figure 11.5.

Thus you can schedule your appointments according to your time, but using the proper scale. So, if a meeting occurs at 9am in one country, you can see that time and see that it is actually a different time in your location. You can use the Swap Time Zones button when you reach your destination to quickly be kept in sync.

Displaying more than one time zone in your calendar can also prove helpful if you work with people in another location. You will know whether you can call or include them in meetings with you over the phone based upon the time difference.

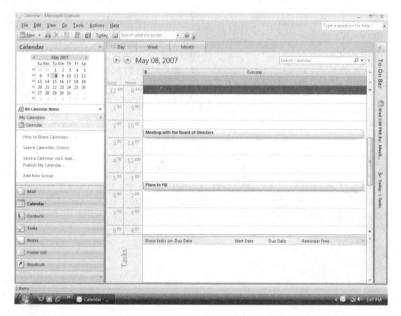

Figure 11.5
Display two time zones.

Important

The only caveat to using Time Zone options is that they can be confusing until you get used to them. And establishing two time zones, although great if you are working with only two locations, proves useless if you are dealing with more than two places.

→ Adding Calendar Items

Now that we know how to navigate and customise our calendar we don't want to forget the most important thing – adding items to our schedule.

There are many ways to add items. You can use the New button off the Standard toolbar, or you can find a date and double-click that date, or you can right-click a day (or time) and find the specific type of item you wish to add. There are three different types of items: appointments, events and meetings.

- Appointments: Have a beginning and ending time and usually occur within a period of the day.

- Events: Are longer episodes that usually span a 24-hour period, like a holiday, business trip, company picnic (really anything that blocks out the entire day).

- Meetings: Allows you to schedule a block of time for a meeting, but also allows you to send that meeting request out to others so they can put it on their calendar.

Creating Our First Appointment

Find the date you wish to add the appointment for and perform the following:

1 Right-click the date and choose "**New Appointment**". Note: If you are in Day view, you can select the exact time for the start of the appointment and it will automatically be added to your appointment item.

2 From the **Appointment** template (shown in Figure 11.6), add the **Subject and Location**.

3 Now select the **Start and End** times. If this is an all-day event, like a planned day off, select the "All day event" checkbox.

4 You can add some notes into the message portion of the template.

5 Select the **Save & Close** option from the Appointment ribbon under the Actions grouping.

11

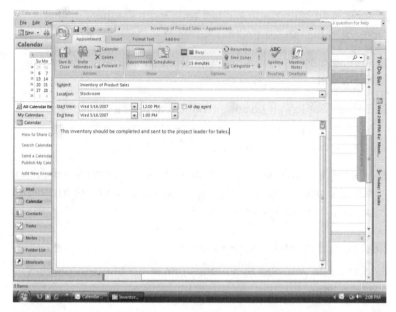

Figure 11.6
Creating an appointment.

Important

Earlier we mentioned that you can use Time Zones when you actually create a message so that Outlook knows which time you really mean, even if you change your system time zone. To do this you have to select the Time Zones button, from the Options grouping off the Appointment ribbon. Then select the down arrows to choose the time zone for your appointment.

When creating an appointment you can also select the **Categorize** option from the **Options** grouping off the Appointment ribbon. Then you can supply a category colour to that appointment.

Timesaver tip

When creating a "New Appointment" or "New Meeting Request", you may type directly in the "Start time" or "End time" date box, text such as "next week" "in two weeks" or "tomorrow". Outlook will recognise the text and voilà, automatically calculate the date for you! In addition, if you type in "noon" in the "time box", 12:00 pm will be entered automatically.

You can also add attachments or contact links. Why would you need attachments? Well, let's say you have an appointment to discuss certain documents. If you include those documents into the appointment, and the contact information of the people you will be holding the appointment with, this centralises all the necessary information in one location. You put it all together when you made the appointment, so you don't have to worry about finding all of that info later on, 5 seconds before the appointment. To add attachments or contact information, go to the Insert ribbon, under the Include grouping, and select Attach File, or Attach Item, or Business Card.

11

Timesaver tip

To quickly create an appointment, based upon an e-mail you receive, you can drag the e-mail from the message pane and place it on the Date Navigator (located on the To-Do Bar). An appointment template will automatically appear asking you to determine the time and date for your appointment. The contents of the e-mail will be included in the appointment's notes section.

Create a Recurring Appointment

Some appointments happen daily, weekly, monthly and so forth. You can establish a recurring appointment by starting from scratch, right-clicking the day and choosing New Recurring Appointment, or from within the Appointment template, selecting the Recurrence button from the Options grouping off the Appointment ribbon. In either case, you will be presented with a scheduler (shown in Figure 11.7).

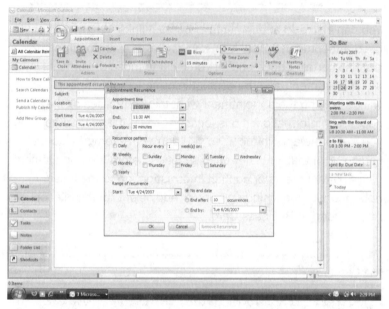

Figure 11.7
Scheduling recurrence of an appointment.

You can confirm the appointment time from within the Appointment Recurrence dialogue and then establish the recurrence pattern. You can configure the following options:

■ Make the appointment daily, weekly, monthly or yearly.

■ Recur every one week (or however many weeks in between the appointment that you decide).

- Recur on a specific day, or multiple days. This is an excellent way to establish an appointment that repeats on (as an example) Monday, Wednesday and Friday.

- Range of recurrence: Decide when to start the recurrence and when to end it (unless you decide that there is no end date). You can end the recurrence after a certain number of times, or when a date is reached.

Create a Meeting

What is the difference between a meeting and an appointment? An appointment is a much looser arrangement to meet with others and take care of specific issues. A meeting requires an organiser and meeting requests go out to the participants for them to accept or decline (or tentatively accept) the invitation. The organiser keeps track of all responses and a reminder is put in all the participants' Outlook calendars. It's quite an advanced method of gathering people.

To begin with, perform the following steps to invite others to a meeting:

11

1 Locate the date on the calendar, right-click that date and choose **New Meeting Request**.

2 From the Meeting Request template, you might notice that you have a To section to include the e-mail addresses of all those you plan to invite to the meeting. Fill in the names (or use the Address Book) to establish your participants.

3 Like an appointment, fill in the subject and location, along with the times. You might include some details about the reason for the meeting, or what you hope to accomplish. You might also include attachments to provide an agenda for the meeting.

4 From the Meeting ribbon, under the Attendees grouping is a **Responses** option. You can "Request Responses" and/or "Allow New Time Proposals".

5 Once the invitation is prepared, select **Send** to send out the meeting invitation.

Sending the invitation is only the first step in making the meeting actually happen. As the sender, you are the organiser too. Once you have the meeting in your calendar, you can check on the progress of responses and add others into the meeting if you like. You can send out update messages (for example, if the time of the meeting has changed). To see more details about your meeting, use your calendar to find the date of the meeting and double-click on it to open up the meeting item.

From the **Meeting** ribbon, under the **Show** grouping, select the **Scheduling** option, shown in Figure 11.8.

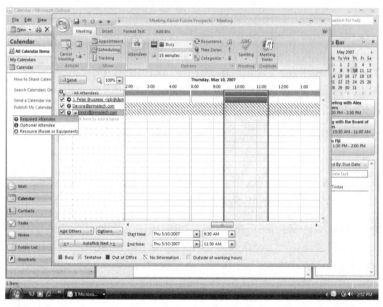

Figure 11.8
Using the meeting planner Scheduling option.

From within the meeting planner you can determine whether you want individuals to be Required or Optional (or responsible for handling the preparation or resources, including perhaps the projector setup and ordering food for the meeting).

You can select the Tracking option to see whether you have received responses from your attendees. This will allow you to send reminders to anyone who hasn't yet responded.

Cancelling a Meeting

If you need to cancel a meeting, you can simply open the meeting reminder off your calendar and select the "**Cancel Meeting**" button from the Actions grouping off the Meeting ribbon. A cancellation message will be prepared to be sent out to all those on the list for attending the meeting. If you hit "**Send Cancellation**" they will all be given an update message that the meeting has been cancelled.

11

12

Collaborating with Others

In this lesson you'll learn how to share, publish, send and print your calendar.

→ Sharing Your Calendar with Others

The Outlook Calendar is a great way to organise your personal schedule, but it goes beyond that. If you work among a team of people whose schedules are an essential part in accomplishing work, you can share your schedule with others who use Outlook.

There are two different ways to share your Calendar – either through an internal exchange server, or through a Microsoft Office Online server to share your schedule over the Internet with friends, family and colleagues who use Outlook.

Another option, if you don't want to work with any servers, is to take a snapshot of your Calendar and send it by e-mail to others to keep them up to date.

Sharing Your Calendar with Exchange

Sharing your calendar in Exchange requires you to alter the permission settings so that you can decide who to share your calendar with. To share your calendar if you are using an exchange server to handle your e-mail, perform the following:

1 From the Navigation pane, right-click the **Calendar** icon and from the options that appear, select **Change Sharing Permissions**.

2 From the **Calendar Properties** dialogue, go to the **Permissions** tab, shown in Figure 12.1.

3 From here you can select the Add button to allow people to have one of ten different permission levels on your calendar.

4 Selecting one of the permission levels alters the corresponding settings in the Read, Write, Delete and Other portions. You can use a predefined permission level such as Editor, Author, Reviewer, and so forth, or you can define a custom set of permissions for the person viewing your calendar.

5 Select OK when you have finished.

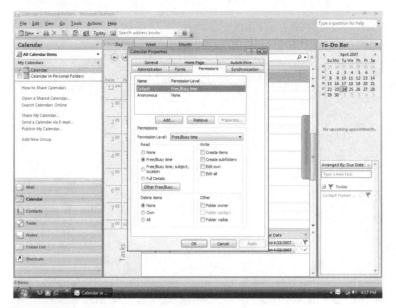

Figure 12.1
Setting permissions for your shared calendar.

Sending Calendar Sharing Invitations

Once you know you have shared a calendar with someone, you
need to let them know. You can do this verbally and they can
connect to your calendar by performing the following:

1 From the Calendar's Navigation pane select the link "**Open a
Shared Calendar**".

2 You will be asked for a name. Note: This is not a name for the
calendar, it's the name of the person whose calendar you
wish to view. You can type it in manually, or you can select
the Name button and choose the name from your contacts.

3 The calendar will now appear alongside your own calendar.

Another way to let people know to access your calendar is by
sending them a message. To do this, right-click the Calendar icon
from the Navigation pane and choose the "**Share Calendar**"
option. The message template, shown in Figure 12.2, has the
checkbox to "Allow recipient to view your Calendar" and another
"Request permission to view recipient's Calendar".

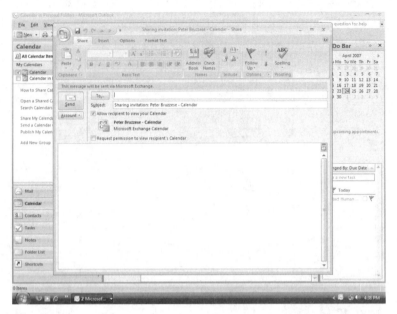

Figure 12.2
Sending an invitation to view your shared calendar.

→ Sharing Your Calendar without Exchange Server

As mentioned above, you can still share your calendar with others, even if they aren't within your company. There are two methods, one involving an online server that you publish your Calendar up to, the other by taking a snapshot of your calendar and sending it by e-mail.

Publishing Your Calendar on the Internet

To publish your Calendar over the Internet you have to create a free Window Live ID. To sign up for this free account, go to the Window Live home site and sign up (https://accountservices. passport.net/ppnetworkhome.srf?lc=1033).

If you already have an account, then to share your calendar, perform the following:

1 From the Navigation pane, right-click the **Calendar** icon.

2 Select **Publish to Internet** and then **Publish to Office Online**. Note: You could also select the Publish My Calendar link from the Navigation pane.

3 Follow the steps of the wizard as it leads you through the Office Online Registration. Note: You will need to register only if it is the first time you are doing this.

4 Once registration is complete, you will be presented with the "Publish Calendar to Microsoft Office Online" dialogue, shown in Figure 12.3.

5 Configure the time span for how much information is shown through your online calendar.

6 Determine the level of detail. There are three settings.

   a Availability only: Time will be shown as Free, Busy, Tentative or Out of the Office.

   b Limited details: Includes the availability and subjects of calendar items only.

   c Full details: Includes the availability and full details of calendar items.

7 Establish permissions, either allowing only those invited to see the calendar or anyone can view and search for the calendar on Office Online.

8 When complete, select OK. You will be asked whether you want to now send an invitation to others about seeing your online calendar. Select Yes if you want others to see your calendar.

9 Provide the e-mail addresses of those you wish to invite and then select **Send**.

12

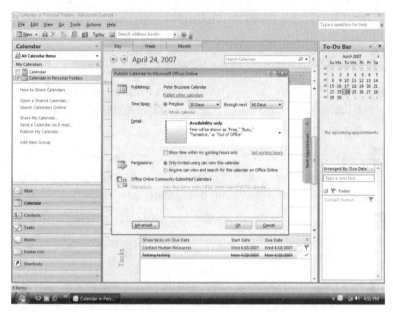

Figure 12.3
Settings for Microsoft Office Online sharing of your calendar.

When the recipient receives the e-mail invitation, they can select the option to subscribe to the calendar and will then be connected to the server and your calendar will become visible on their screen.

Sending a Calendar in E-mail

If you don't feel it's absolutely necessary for people to be that involved in your schedule, but you want them to see a quick snapshot of your calendar, you can send it as a file in .ics format. The caveat here is that people will not be able to make changes to it and it isn't automatically updated, but it's quick and easy and you can send manual updates if you like. Plus, the .ics calendar file is not used only in Outlook but in many scheduling programs, so it's almost guaranteed that the recipient will be able to open it, even if they don't use Outlook.

To send a calendar using e-mail, perform the following:

1 From the Navigation pane, right-click the **Calendar** icon and select **Send via E-mail**. Or, you can select the **Send a Calendar via E-mail** link off the Navigation pane.

2 An e-mail message template will open and a Send a Calendar via E-mail dialogue will open in the centre, as shown in Figure 12.4.

3 If you have more than one calendar (perhaps one on the exchange server and one in your personal folders) you can select which one you want to use.

4 Configure the Date Range as to how much you wish to show of your schedule.

5 Select the level of details you wish to show (much like you did when you published the Calendar).

6 If you wish to e-mail only your working hour time you can select the checkbox "Show time within my working hours only".

7 Then hit OK.

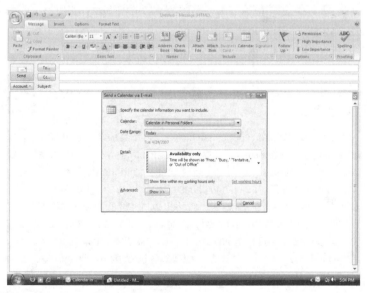

Figure 12.4
Send a calendar via e-mail.

Once you have your options configured, you only have to add the
people you wish to e-mail it to and click Send. People will receive
an e-mail with an .ics attached calendar that should display
easily, as we see in Figure 12.5.

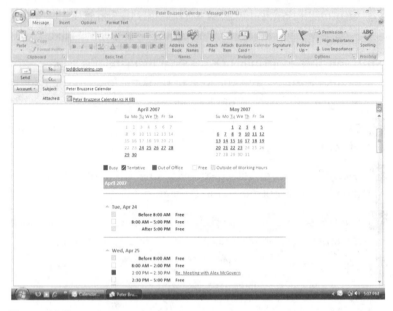

Figure 12.5
An e-mail with calendar included.

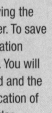

Important

Another way to share your schedule via the Internet is by saving the
calendar as an .html file and then uploading it to a web server. To save
your calendar in this way, select the calendar from the Navigation
pane. Select the **File** menu and choose **Save As Web Page**. You will
be asked how much of your calendar you want to have saved and the
detail levels (if you want to include a background) and the location of
the page created. Select **Save** and now you have your calendar
available to post to your web server. It won't be dynamically updated,
so remember to make updates from time to time.

→ Printing Your Calendar

Even with all our modern gadgets, there is nothing wrong with wanting your schedule in the palm of your hand, literally (and we aren't talking about on a mobile PC). Nope – good old-fashioned paper. Ahem... with a printed calendar from a high-end colour laser jet printer. Yes! We can rough it a little just like the early explorers!

To print your calendar you simply need to select it and then select the **File** menu, then **Print**. The Print dialogue, shown in Figure 12.6, will provide you with the opportunity to choose a print style (be it daily, weekly, monthly, tri-fold or calendar details) and a print range (where you can determine the start and end date for your printed calendar. You can even opt to "Hide details of private appointments".

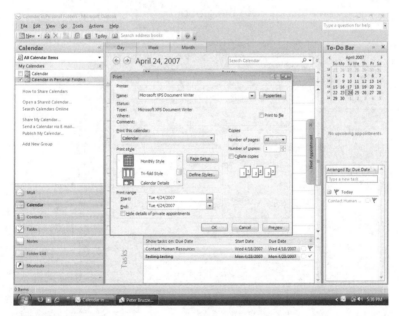

Figure 12.6
Printing a calendar.

→ Group Scheduling

Sharing your schedule with others may be helpful at times; however, you may want to view the schedule of an entire team of people. If you work with a team who all have accounts on the exchange server within your company, you can create a group schedule.

To create a group schedule, perform the following:

1 From the Calendar view, select the **View Group Schedules** button on the Standard toolbar.

2 From the Group Schedules dialogue, select the **New** button and provide a name for the group.

3 From within the scheduling window, as shown in Figure 12.7, you can add others to the group.

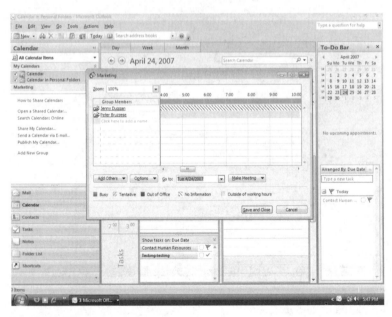

Figure 12.7
Group scheduling.

You can select the Make Meeting button to easily invite others to a meeting. From the Meeting Maker you will be able to see everyone's schedule and thus determine a good time for the meeting. Or you could just select the **Make Meeting** button and choose the **New Mail Message** option.

Important

One important factor to consider when using Exchange and sharing out your calendar is that other people within your company may use that information (the free/busy information) to determine times for meetings. So, you need to be conscientious about keeping your calendar up to date, otherwise you appear to have more free time in your schedule than you do.

12

13

Organising Schedules with Tasks and the To-Do Bar

In this lesson you'll learn about working with the To-Do Bar and Tasks.

→ Working with the To-Do Bar

Tasks and To-Do items are not the same thing. The To-Do Bar contains any Outlook item, be it a message, tasks, contact that has been flagged for follow-up, as shown in Figure 13.1. Note: We discussed flagging items in Chapter 10. All flagged items show up in your To-Do Bar in the order from first to last, or last to first (you can configure this by selecting the down arrow on the To-Do Bar and choosing the up or down arrow).

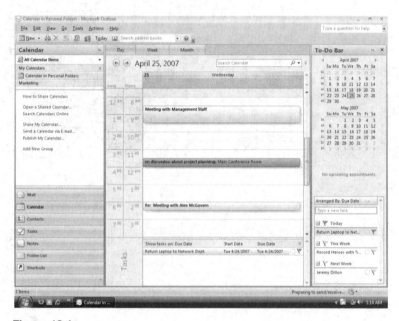

Figure 13.1
The To-Do Bar.

Your To-Do list is located on the right-hand side and you can turn it off, set it to be minimised or leave it showing normally. The three primary portions of the To-Do Bar are the Date Navigator, Appointments and Tasks List. You can turn off any of these by selecting the Views menu, pointing to the To-Do Bar and de-selecting any of the controls.

Timesaver tip

If you want to see more than one Date Navigator in the To-Do Bar, you can do this by selecting the **Views** menu, pointing to the **To-Do Bar**, selecting **Options** and then increasing the "Number of month rows" to 2 or 3 (however many you need and have room for).

While it's easy to see your appointments and calendars when you are working in those folders, if you find yourself, like most people, working in the Mail folder, it's the To-Do Bar that will keep you in touch with your appointments and tasks. The To-Do Bar is your connection to those other portions of Outlook.

→ Working with Tasks

Tasks are items that you create in Outlook that you can track to completion. These tasks could include simple items like a note to yourself, or more complex items like an appointment that you've scheduled.

When you select the Task folder off the Navigation pane, you are presented with what looks like a duplicate of the To-Do Bar. This is because your view may have "To-Do List" selected under Current View. There are actually 13 different views to choose from and some of them can be quite detailed and informative. You can see tasks that you've assigned to others as well and see those that have been completed. Try the different views to see which ones may help you be more productive.

13

For example:

■ The Active Tasks view allows you to see all tasks that aren't completed or deferred.

- The Next Seven Days view lets you see views that will be due over the next seven days (although it doesn't show you overdue tasks).

- Overdue Tasks shows you the overdue tasks.

- By Category lets you see tasks according to the categories you have assigned.

- Assignment and By Person views come in handy if you have assigned tasks to others. (We will discuss this shortly, it's called "delegating!")

- Completed Tasks lets you see those tasks that are behind you now. Sometimes it's good to see what you've accomplished.

Create a Task

When you create a calendar appointment, this becomes part of your tasks for that day. You can create a task directly from the To-Do Bar, or by using the Tasks selection off the Navigation pane.

To create a task that has to be carried out today, perform the following:

1 From the To-Do Bar or the Tasks pane, select the input box that has the words "Type a new task" in light grey. Type the task you need accomplished and hit **Enter**.

2 Now the task is created. If you double-click the task, you can enter the task template window, shown in Figure 13.2, and make changes to the task.

3 When your task is established, select **Save & Close**.

To create a new task that has more detail to it, perform the following:

1 From the **Tasks** folder, select **New** (or New, then New Task). Or you can hit **Ctrl+Shift+K**.

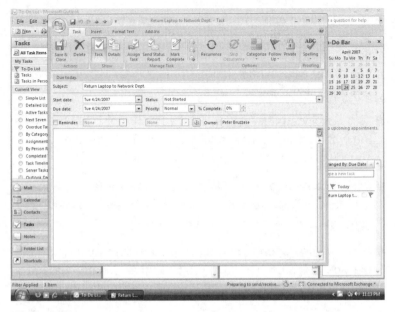

Figure 13.2
Creating tasks.

2 From the task template window you can add a subject, a start and due date, assign a status and priority (low, normal, high), or even indicate a percentage complete.

   a The Status and % Complete are linked. 0% is "Not Started", 1–99% is "In Progress", 100% is "Completed".

   b If you send the task to someone else, it will show up as Deferred. You can also select "Waiting on someone else".

3 When your task is established, select **Save & Close**.

Working with Task Options

The Task ribbon offers you a variety of options to use in order to make the tasks you create a productive tool. Here are some of the options you can configure within a task:

- To add more information to a task, especially upon completion, select the **Details** button from the **Show** grouping on the Task ribbon. From here you can configure the date completed, total and actual work in hours, mileage (if you were required to drive) and billing information.

- To be reminded of a task, select the **Reminder** checkbox from the main task template window and determine the time and sound you want to hear.

- Select the **Assign Task** button, located on the Task ribbon in the Manage Task grouping, to send off the task you create to someone else. This is the ultimate in delegating.

- Send **Status Report** button located on the Task ribbon in the Manage Task grouping allows you to send an update message on the status of the task, including a percentage level of completion.

- Mark Complete button located on the Task ribbon in the Manage Task grouping makes the task vanish quickly. But it is still remembered and will show up again if you select the Completed Tasks view.

- Categorize, Follow Up and Private: These settings are all found under the Options grouping off the Task ribbon and they function the same way here as they do in other aspects of Outlook. You can place this task within a category. For example, if the task is to pick up milk on the way home, you might place this under your "Personal" category. Follow Up places a flag to the message for you to track the task easily and follow up on its completion. Marking it as Private will prevent others from seeing the details if they have shared access to your Tasks folder.

→ Recurring Tasks

Unlike appointments, events or meetings, which may or may not have a pattern to them, tasks can often be recurring. For example, some people take vitamins each day and need a little reminder. You can set up a task that prompts you to take them. Some tasks might help you perform your job better, such as keeping in touch with a client by setting up a task to check in with them at specified intervals.

To set up a recurring task, perform the following:

1 Create your task and fill in the details, including the subject and any details in the notes pane.

13

2 Then select the **Recurrence** button from the **Options** grouping off the Task ribbon. The Task Recurrence dialogue box appears, as shown in Figure 13.3.

3 You can establish the following options:

a Make the task daily, weekly, monthly or yearly.

b Recurrence options vary depending on your first choice. You can define the interval for a recurring task. For example, if you select Monthly, you can schedule the task to be scheduled on a specific day each month, or on the "fourth Wednesday of every month" or "of every 2 months" and so forth. Your options for scheduling are quite extensive.

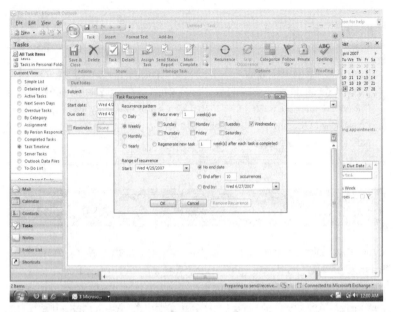

Figure 13.3
The Task Recurrence dialogue box.

c Regenerate New Task is an interesting option. This allows
you to schedule a task and set the recurrence in such a way
that you schedule the recurrence to happen after you
complete the last task. This can come in really handy. Let's
say you want to call your client once a month. So you have
a task schedule for the 1st of the month. But let's say you
try your client and it takes a couple of weeks before you
finally connect. If you have a task scheduled on the 1st of
the month, you will be looking to call him pretty soon. You
might begin to irritate the client. With the Regenerate New
Task options, you can configure the schedule to dynamically
work from when you complete the last task. If you finally
contact your client on the 15th, it will schedule your next
call for the 15th of the following month, not the 1st.

d Range of recurrence: Decide when to start the recurrence
and when to end it (unless you decide that there is no end
date). You can end the recurrence after a certain number of
times, or when a date is reached.

14

Using Outlook Contacts

In this lesson you'll learn about working with Contacts in Outlook 2007.

→ The Contacts Folder

Your Contacts folder is your repository for all your connections. You can create contacts that contain only a name and e-mail, or contacts that contain everything from a person's name and address, to their favourite donut. This database of information can also include photos of the contact (if you have them) so you won't forget a face. It's imperative that you use the Contacts folder to really keep track of your contact information. Dale Carnegie (motivational speaker and author of *How to Win Friends and Influence People*) said: "You can close more business in two months by becoming interested in other people than you can in two years by trying to get people interested in you." That is excellent advice when thinking about the contacts we keep. There is even a notes section so that you can indicate how a person took their coffee, what type of sandwich they liked, perhaps some points about their likes and dislikes. True, this in-depth information isn't necessary for each person you meet, but it's a good habit to get into in business.

OK, now that you are excited about using Contacts, let's get started.

Creating a New Contact

We discussed this briefly in Chapter 7, but let's go over the creation of a contact in greater detail. To begin with, select the Contacts folder. The default is the Business Cards view, shown in Figure 14.1.

You can select another view – there are eight different ones to choose from. Some of these views can prove very helpful in quickly finding specific people. For example, let's say you need to speak to someone in Company A. You have hundreds of different people in your Contacts, how will you find them all? Simply select the By Company view and you can see all your contacts grouped by their company. If your first contact at Company A doesn't work, move on to the next one in your list.

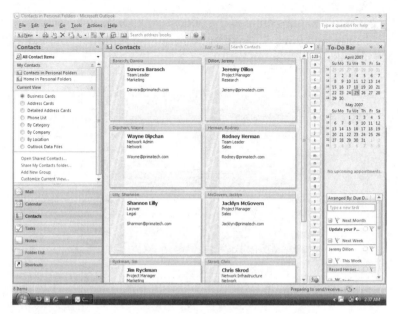

Figure 14.1
Contacts in the Business Card view.

You can also organise your contacts by category and then use the By Category option to break your contacts into their categories. The organisational benefits are unbelievable.

To create a new contact, perform the following:

1 From within the **Contacts** folder, select **New** and the **New Contact Template** will appear, as shown in Figure 14.2. (Note: You can also hit **Ctrl+Shift+C** or from the File menu, select New, then Contact.)

2 Begin in the first field and use the tab button to move from one field to the next, or use your mouse to select specific fields you wish to fill in.

3 The fields you are filling in are the most common fields for information about a person. However, on the **Contact** ribbon, under the **Show** grouping, you can select the **All Fields** button to see the more than 140 fields that each contact has, as shown in Figure 14.3.

14

4 Once you have entered the necessary information you can select the **Save & Close** option from the **Actions** grouping off the **Contact** ribbon.

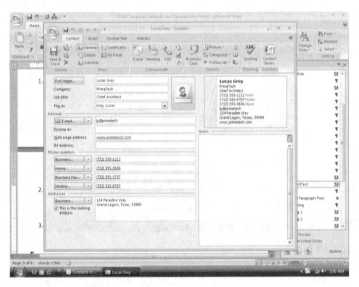

Figure 14.2
Creating a Contact.

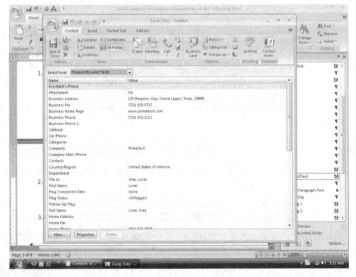

Figure 14.3
Adding more information to a contact through the All Fields button.

Important

You can use these contacts to perform other tasks such as mail merges, or addressing letters and envelopes. To do that you will use the fields we are discussing here. The name fields especially are important and you need to know how Outlook breaks up the name you put in the Full Name field. Select the Full Name button from the Contacts template and you will see each field used to make up the name, as shown in Figure 14.4.

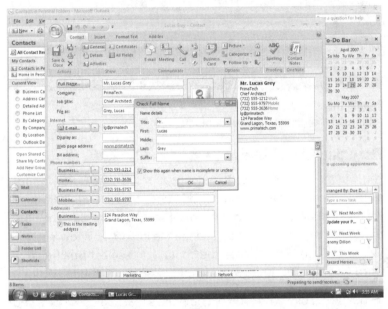

Figure 14.4
The Full Name button shows you the details.

If you want to add more details to your contact, select the Details button, located on the Contact ribbon, under the Show grouping. The Details options allow you to configure information about the contact such as his/her business information (like department and manager's name) along with personal information (like nickname, spouse/partner and birthday or anniversary), as shown in Figure 14.5.

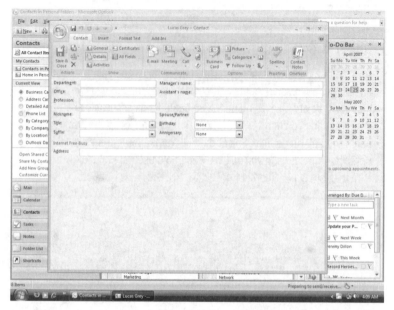

Figure 14.5
Adding further details to your contacts.

Changing the Business Card

You can make a variety of changes to the Business Card view for
a contact. For example, you can add and remove certain fields
you want displayed. You can align the text differently, change the
background colour and even change the image, as shown in
Figure 14.6. To do this, open the contact and select **Business
Card** from the **Options** grouping off the **Contact** ribbon.

If you have a digital version of someone's real business card, you
can use it as the background for the card itself, adding a nice
graphic to the card. Or, if you have a picture of the individual, you
can select the Picture button on the Options grouping and include
the picture. It's easy to "never forget a face" when you have that
face included with the contacts.

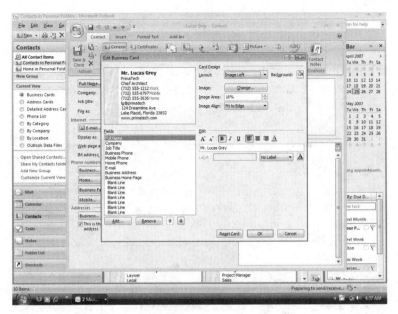

Figure 14.6
Changing the Business Card features.

→ Using Contacts to Communicate

Once you have a contact in your Contacts folder, you can locate that contact and double-click it to bring up all its details. Once the contact is open you can perform the following tasks from the Communicate grouping located on the Contact ribbon.

14

- E-mail: Creates a new mail message with the contact's e-mail address already included.

- Meeting: Establishes a new meeting request with the contact's e-mail address already included and the ability for you to fill in the meeting information.

- Call: Allows you to place a call to the contact (using one of the phone numbers of your choosing).

- Assign Task: Allows you to delegate a task to the contact.

- Web Page: Brings you to the web page of the contact, if they have one listed.

- Map: Takes the address you have given and reaches out to MSN Maps & Directions site on the Internet and provides you with a map of the address for your contact.

Timesaver tip

Using the Map option is a great time saver because you may need to locate your contact and this quickly brings you to his/her address. You can also request directions off the MSN page.

→ Printing Contacts

The options you are shown when printing contacts depends on the view you are using. For example, if you are using the Business Card view you will have the options shown in Figure 14.7, which offer different styles. If you are viewing your cards in Lists or Categories view, you will be shown only table styles when printing from lists or category views (which may be what you need for creating a phone list).

Before printing, select the **Preview** button to make sure the style is what you are looking for. If not, select the **Page Setup** button to bring you to the formatting options, shown in Figure 14.8.

Figure 14.7
Printing styles for cards.

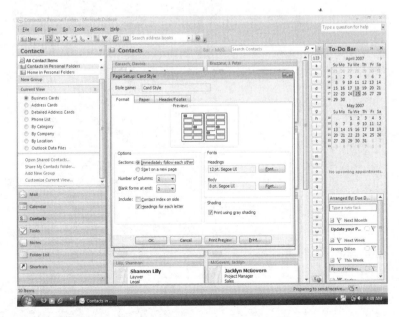

Figure 14.8
Print formatting.

14

15

Using Outlook's RSS Feeds

In this lesson you'll be introduced to Really Simple Syndication (RSS) and learn how to access, read and manage RSS Feeds.

→ What is RSS?

Jargon buster

RSS has several terms associated with it, including Really Simple Syndication, Rich Site Summary or RDF Summary. Generally, though, the acronym stands for Really Simple Syndication.

Essentially, RSS is a web feed format that publishes out digital content (like news or blog sites) that users can subscribe to and read through feed readers, as opposed to navigating to a person's website to read the latest news. The reader checks to see whether there are any new entries on the RSS feeds and then retrieves those new entries.

One of the great benefits to an RSS feed that is pulled in by a reader is that you don't have to visit several sites to gather the latest information from a variety of locations. You can establish connections to RSS sites and summaries of the contents will be sent to you as a link and you can decide whether you want to read those articles based upon clicking the link.

Outlook 2007 is an RSS aggregator. It allows a user to organise their RSS feeds and check on them for new content.

→ Accessing RSS Feeds

You may be wondering, "where do I find these RSS feeds?" Well, when you go to various websites, you might see certain icons like the following: , **RSS** or **XML** .

When you select these icons you can subscribe to the feed from your web browser. However, you may want to add a feed into

Outlook. To do this you can perform a search on the Internet for places that have RSS feeds.

Once you find a site that you want to include in your feeds, perform the following:

1 Select the **Tools** menu, **Accounts Settings** option.

2 Select the **RSS Feeds** tab, shown in Figure 15.1.

3 Click **New** and type in the path to the RSS feed.

4 Select **Add**.

5 You can make some changes from the RSS Feed Options dialogue, shown in Figure 15.2. Generally, the default settings are fine.

6 Select **OK and Close**.

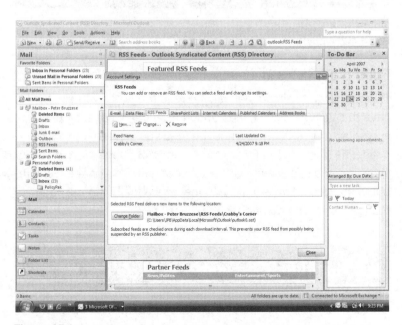

Figure 15.1
Subscribe to a feed.

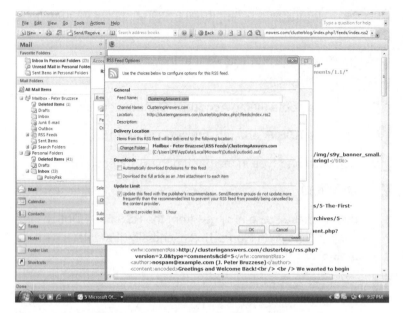

Figure 15.2
RSS Feed Options.

Read the RSS Feed

This part is quite simple actually. To read the feeds you simply have to select the RSS Feeds option from the Navigation pane and select the folder that holds the feed you wish to read. You'll notice, as illustrated in Figure 15.3, that RSS Feeds will typically show you the information you would normally find on the website, but in the form of an e-mail, with the difference being the little orange icon in the corner of each message.

→ Managing RSS Feeds

One concern you might have with RSS Feeds is how often it checks for new content. Each site is different. If it's news, you could get several updates an hour. If it's a blog, you might get one update per day. You can see what the setting is for your particular feed by returning to the Tools, Account Settings, RSS Feeds tab.

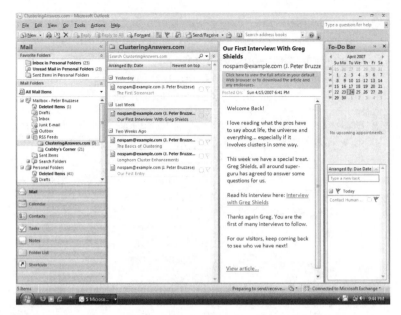

Figure 15.3
Reading an RSS feed item.

Select the specific feed you are interested in and then choose the **Change** option.

You will see under the Update Limit that there is a selection that says "Update this feed with the publisher's recommendation. Send/Receive groups do not update more frequently than the recommended limit to prevent your RSS feed from possibly being cancelled by the content provided". And then you will be shown the provider limit.

If there is no specified limit, then the Send/Receive setting for the RSS Feed is used. To check/modify this setting, perform the following:

1 First, go to the **Tools** menu, point to **Send/Receive**, then point to **Send/Receive Settings** and finally select **Define Send/Receive Groups**.

15

2 Your RSS feeds are located within one of the groups. Most likely you have just one grouping called **All Accounts**. If you select that group you can choose **Edit** and you will see your various account settings, as shown in Figure 15.4. RSS is located, by default, in the All Accounts group.

3 Under the setting "Schedule an automatic send/receive every xx minutes" (the default is 30), you can change the time.

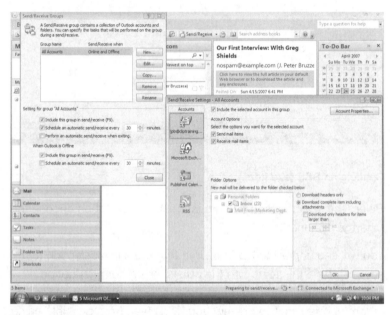

Figure 15.4
Configuring Send/Receive options.

Important

If you select a time interval that is more frequent than the publisher, Outlook will use the publisher's setting. If you connect too frequently to an RSS feed, the publisher may ban you from the site.

Change the Folder to Which an RSS Feed is Delivered

The RSS Feed folder located at the root of your folder structure is a fine place for all your feeds to be located. However, you may need to have certain feeds sent to a different location. From the Account Settings, the RSS Feeds tab, you can select the Change Folder button. This will give you the option to alter where your Feed is sent, as shown in Figure 15.5. This will take you to the New RSS Feed Delivery Location.

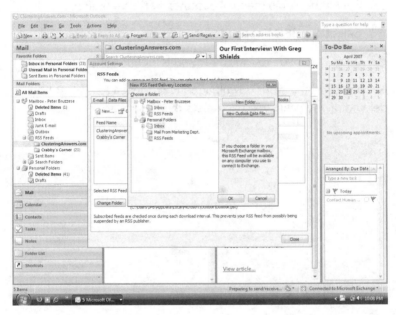

Figure 15.5
Changing the folder for your RSS feed.

From here you can have your feed sent to a different folder, you can create new folders, or create a new Outlook .pst file for your feed. Keep in mind, however, that if you keep your RSS Feed with your exchange server, you can access it from any Outlook client you use that is connected to the same server. If you bring your feeds down to the personal folders into a .pst file, you will lighten the amount of data kept on the exchange server, but you will be able to see those feeds only if you are on the system where the .pst file resides.

15

Jargon buster

.pst file A file extension for Personal File Folders.

Deleting Feeds

To delete a feed, perform the following:

1 Select the **Tools** menu, **Accounts Settings** option.

2 Select the **RSS Feeds** tab.

3 Click **Remove**. You will be asked to confirm the decision.

Keep in mind that your downloaded RSS messages will not be deleted. If you wish, you can delete them manually.

Overview of Word 2007

16

Familiarising Yourself with Word

In this lesson you'll learn how to open, close and customise Word. You'll also learn how to use the Word Ribbon.

The Word program in Microsoft Office is used for word processing. You can enter and save text and add text, pictures, graphs and colours. This chapter covers the basics of Word as well as some of the more in-depth activities such as adding visual appeal, proofreading and Quick Parts.

→ Opening Word

Opening Word is a simple four-step process:

1 Click the **Windows** Button.

2 Select **All Programs**.

3 Select **Microsoft Office**.

4 Click **Microsoft Word 2007**.

This opens Word to a blank document (see Figure 16.1).

Figure 16.1
A new Word document.

After you open the same Office program once or twice, the icon for that program appears on your Start menu. When the icon is there, you can just click that icon instead of going through the All Programs menu to get to the program.

You can also create a shortcut for Word, allowing you to open it from the desktop. Use the following steps to place a shortcut icon on your desktop:

1 Click the **Windows** Button.

2 Choose **All Programs**.

3 Select **Microsoft Office**.

4 Right-click **Microsoft Word 2007** – this brings up a drop-down menu, shown in Figure 16.2.

5 Click **Send To** and select **Desktop**. A shortcut icon for Word appears on your desktop.

Then, to open Word from the desktop icon, double-click the icon.

Figure 16.2
Word Drop-Down Menu

→ Using the Word Ribbon

Once you become familiar with the Word Ribbon (see Figure 16.3) it is easy to use. Keep in mind when using any Ribbon that the contextual tabs are titled with a category and the category titles are the keyword to what commands the tabs will contain.

Figure 16.3
The Word ribbon is much different from previous versions of Word.

There are eight contextual tabs in the Word Ribbon. Here is a brief overview of the commands that each tab contains:

- **Home**. The Home tab contains the most popular commands used in Word. There is the clipboard, for cutting, copying and pasting; font selections; paragraph formatting options; styles; and editing, which allows you to find, replace and select text.

- **Insert**. The Insert tab gives you the commands you need to insert certain graphics, objects and elements into your document, including a cover page, table, pictures, art, charts, symbols and even a signature line.

- **Page Layout**. The Page Layout tab contains the commands for themes, page setup, page background, paragraph and arrange.

- **References**. The References tab has the commands that enable you to create a table of contents, footnotes, citations and bibliography, captions, index and table of authorities.

- **Mailings**. The Mailings tab is where you look for mail-related commands such as mail merge and creating envelopes and labels.

- **Review**. The Review tab contains the spelling and grammar check and the thesaurus. You will also find commands for proofing, comments, tracking, changes, compare and protect.

- **View**. The View tab contains the commands used to change your document view, customise your document window, zoom and access macros.

- **Add-Ins**. The Add-Ins tab is where you can access and manage document add-ins.

Although the Ribbon and tab scheme makes Word look much different from the past, once you familiarise yourself with it, you'll find that it actually makes work flow much better. And if you've used Word before, you should be able to familiarise yourself with it in less than an hour.

→ Changing Your View

16

One feature you might find useful is the ability to change the way you view a document in Word. This helps with editing or proofing tasks and it allows you to work in an orientation that's comfortable for you. Use these steps to change your view:

1 Select the **View tab** in the Word Ribbon.

2 From the **Document Views** section of the Ribbon on the far left side, select the viewing layout that meets your needs.

3 At any time you can go back to the View tab and change your view to another one if you're not comfortable in the one you are using.

As Figure 16.4 shows, you have several document views, the option to show or hide certain tools for your document, zoom options, window options and Macros.

Figure 16.4
View ribbon.

Here's how you use those commands:

■ **Document Views**. This gives you five different ways you can view a document:

 – The Print Layout view is the default view and will be how you see a document when you first open Word.

 – The Full Screen Reading will let you see your document pages side by side and turn them as you would pages in a book.

 – The web Layout lets you view your document as you would a web page.

 – The Outline and Draft views let you view your document in an outline or draft format.

- **Show/Hide**. These commands let you choose the tools that you can see when you are working on an open document.

- **Zoom**. The Zoom commands let you change how large or small your document view is, how many pages you see at a time and what the page width will be.

- **Windows**. This allows you to customise how you view your windows.

- **Macros**. This is where you will find your macro options.

You can use any of these commands to change the view of your document to better suit your needs.

→ Saving Files and Closing Word

Saving files in Word has changed somewhat from previous versions of Microsoft Office. There are several ways to save a Word document:

- The keyboard combination **Ctrl+S** saves your document with an existing file name. If the document does not already have a name, it saves the document by number – Document 1, Document 2, etc.

- Selecting the **Diskette** icon next to the Office Button saves your document with an existing file name. If the document does not already have a name, it saves the document by number – Document 1, Document 2, etc.

- Selecting the **Office** button opens a drop-down menu, from which you can select **Save** or **Save As** and enter the document name when prompted, as shown in Figure 16.5.

16

Figure 16.5
Save As menu

→ Customising Word

If you are not comfortable with the layout of Word, you can customise the window to be more user friendly. There are several things that you can customise in Word:

- **Quick Access Toolbar**. Next to the Quick Access Toolbar, which is located to the right of the Windows Button, is a down-pointing arrow that gives you a drop-down menu which allows you to customise the toolbar, as shown in Figure 16.6.

  You can select or deselect the items that you would or wouldn't like to have available in the toolbar. You can also choose to show your Quick Access toolbar below the Ribbon from this menu.

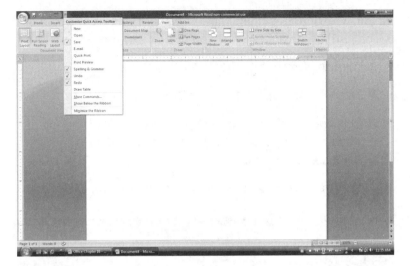

Figure 16.6
Quick Access Toolbar Customise Window.

■ **The Ribbon:** If you are not comfortable with the Ribbon in view, or if you need more window space to work, you can minimise the Ribbon. There are two ways to do this. Option one is a two-step process:

1 Click the down arrow in the Quick Access Toolbar.

2 From the drop-down menu, select **Minimize Ribbon**.

To make the Ribbon reappear, click any of the menu commands at the top of the page. The Ribbon will then remain available until it has been idle for a few seconds, at which time it hides away again.

Option two hides the Ribbon, except for the contextual tabs:

1 Double-click an open contextual tab.

2 To make it reappear, do the same thing.

16

■ **Further Customisation:** There are other customisation options in Word too. To access those options, follow these steps:

1 Click the Office Button.

2 From the pop-up menu, select **Word Options**.

3 This opens the menu, as shown in Figure 16.7. Browse through the options on the left side of the menu, selecting the areas to customise.

4 Once you have finished customising Word, click **OK**.

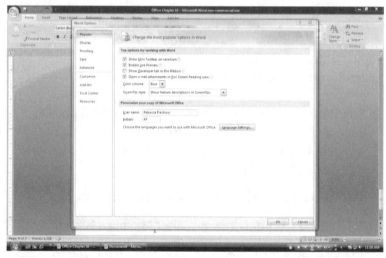

Figure 16.7
Word Options menu.

17

Getting Started with Word Documents

In this lesson you'll learn how to start, open, save and close Word documents.

→ Starting and Opening Documents

Now that you are familiar with how to open and customise Word and how to use the Ribbon, it's time to start using Word to create documents and publications. To start a document from a blank page in Word (seen in Figure 17.1), you simply have to open Word and start typing.

Figure 17.1
Microsoft Word blank document.

Creating a document is easy. But you won't always be creating documents. There will be times when you're opening existing documents that you or someone else has created. To open an existing document in Word:

1 Click the **Windows** Button.

2 In the menu that appears, select **Open**.

3 Navigate to the location in which the existing document is stored. Usually, this will be in the My Documents folder, shown in Figure 17.2.

4 Select the file you want and click **Open**. This opens the
document in a new Word window.

Figure 17.2
My Documents.

Timesaver tip

Instead of selecting the file you want to open and clicking Open, you
can just double-click on the file name.

You can also open a document that you've accessed recently
from the Word program. To open recent documents, follow
these steps:

1 Open Microsoft Word 2007.

2 Click the **Office** Button.

3 From the **Recent Documents** list on the right side of the
menu that appears, as shown in Figure 17.3, select the
document you would like to open.

17

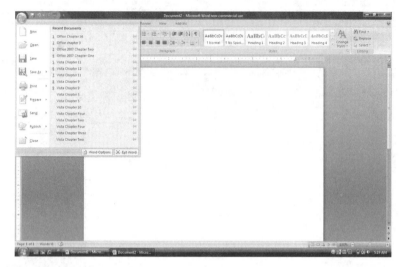

Figure 17.3
Office Button pop-up menu.

Important

Only the last 17 documents that you've accessed will appear in this menu. If you've opened more than 17 documents since the last time you accessed the desired file, it will not appear in this list. You can also pin a document to the list so that it will always appear there by clicking the pushpin to the right of the document name. When you're ready to unpin that document, click the pushpin icon again.

→ Adding Text to Your Document

Once you have an open document, you can start adding text. Text is anything from a simple word to several paragraphs or pages of words. To add text to a Word document, put your cursor anywhere on the page and start typing.

You can also insert a text box into your document to change the direction of your text, or to add more visual appeal to the document. A text box allows you to type text that is not part of the main body of the document.

To insert a text box into your document, follow these steps:

1 Create or open a Word document.

2 Go to the **Insert** tab.

3 In the **Text** section of the Ribbon, select **Text Box**. As shown in Figure 17.4, a menu of sidebars and text boxes appears.

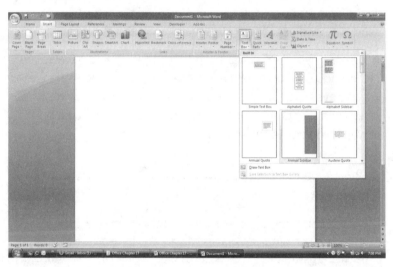

Figure 17.4
The menu of sidebars and text boxes.

4 Select the text box you would like to use. It is automatically entered into your document. You can then reposition the text box if desired. When you do, text within your document will be automatically formatted to flow around the text box.

5 If there is not a text box you like in the existing selection, you can select **Draw Text Box**. This turns your pointer into a drawing tool and you can draw a text box within your document at any location and in any size that suits you.

6 When you've finished inserting the text box into your document, the Ribbon will automatically switch to a hidden, contextual tab – the **Text Box Tools** tab. This tab provides all the tools you need to create interesting, appealing text boxes.

→ Saving and Closing Documents

Once you have used Microsoft Office 2007 Word to create documents and publications, you can save them for future accessing and use. There are several ways to save a file:

■ You can use the keyboard shortcut **Ctrl+S**. If you have saved the document before then it will be resaved to the same file. If you have never saved that document, however, a window appears that prompts you to choose a name and location to which you would like to save the file.

Important

Word periodically creates a temporary save of your document that serves as a backup to protect you in the event of the program crashing before you have saved the file on which you are working. The saved document is temporary, however, and when you close out of Word without saving your document, even this temporary file is lost. It's best if you get into the habit of saving your document every 5–10 minutes while you're working.

■ If you try to close a Word document without saving it, a pop-up message appears on the screen prompting you to save your changes, as shown in Figure 17.5. Select **Yes** and the **Save As** dialogue box appears so you can enter a file name and select a location to which you'd like to save the file. When you've entered this information, click **Save**.

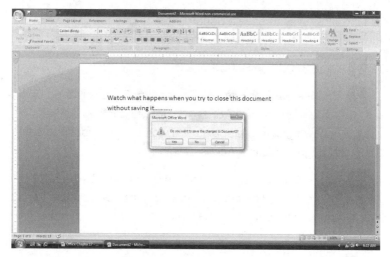

Figure 17.5
Save Document prompt.

■ You can also save a document from the Quick Access Toolbar. To do this, click on the disk icon in the toolbar. This will bring up the menu shown in Figure 17.6. From the left of the menu, choose the folder or program you would like to save your document in, enter the file name and click **Save**.

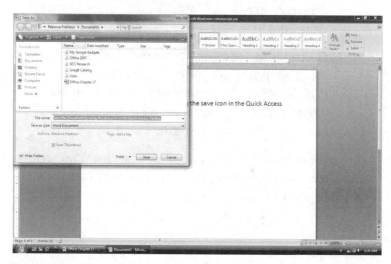

Figure 17.6
Save menu.

■ One other way to save a document is to use the Office Button menu. Here are the steps to save a document using that menu:

1 Click the Office Button.

2 Choose Save or Save As – choosing Save will bring up the same menu as in 17.6, as will double-clicking Save As. Follow the same steps as you would if you chose to save through the Quick Access Toolbar.

3 If you choose Save As, a menu will appear to the right (see Figure 17.7). There are several options you can use to save your document:

- **Word Document**. This will save your document in the default format.

- **Word Template**. If you save a copy of your document as a Word template, you will be able to access it in the future as a template for other documents. This allows you to apply the same formatting and style options that are used in the original document.

- **Word 97–2003**. Choosing this save option creates a document that is compatible with previous versions of Word from 97–2003.

- **Find add-ins for other file formats**. This option allows you to save your document in other formats, such as PDF or XPS. To save documents in these formats, however, you must download the add-ins from the Microsoft Office Online website.

- **Other Formats**. This option will open the Save As menu and allows you to select from all file types, as shown in Figure 17.7.

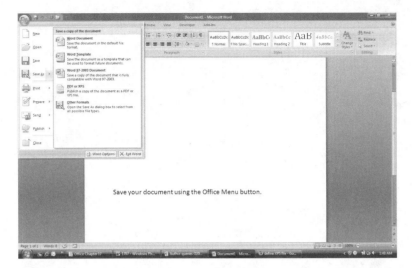

Figure 17.7
Save As options.

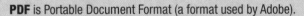

Jargon buster

PDF is Portable Document Format (a format used by Adobe).

XPS is an XML Paper Specification file which is essentially a zipped archive file.

Once you have saved your document, you can close Word without losing your work. There are two ways to close Word:

■ Click the **close button (X)** in the top right corner of the window.

■ Click the **Office Button** and select **Close** at the bottom of the menu.

The Word program closes and you are returned to your desktop or to another application window that you might have open.

17

18

Editing Your Documents

In this lesson you'll learn about working with text in your documents and how to add, replace, rearrange, move, select and delete it.

→ Adding, Replacing and Rearranging Text

When you are creating a document in Microsoft Office Word, there are times that you want to add text here, delete text there or move something to a completely different spot. Fortunately, these tasks are easy to perform in Word 2007.

There are a few ways to add text to a document. You can always place your cursor anywhere within a document and start typing at that location. Remember to pay close attention to spacing when you are adding text, especially in the middle of a sentence or paragraph.

Replacing text in Word is simple, too. The easiest way to do this is to use the Find and Replace Tool (see Figure 18.1).

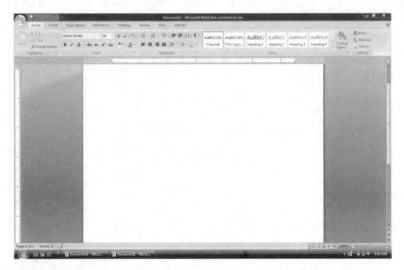

Figure 18.1
Find and Replace tool.

There are two ways to open the Find and Replace Tool:

1 From the **Home** tab on the Ribbon, there is an Editing box (as seen in Figure 18.1). From the Editing box, select **Replace**. This opens the **Find and Replace** dialogue box, shown in Figure 18.2.

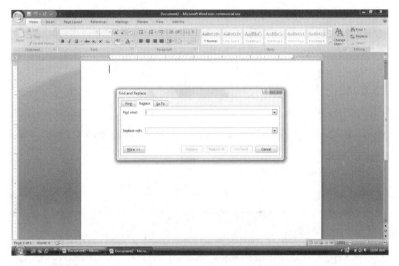

Figure 18.2
Find and Replace box.

2 At the bottom of the scroll bar is a set of up and down arrows with a button between them. This is the **Browser** Objects button. Select it to open a menu of Browser Objects, as shown in Figure 18.3. Select the picture of the binoculars, which opens the **Find and Replace** dialogue box. Click the Replace tab and then type the word you want to replace in the **Find what** box and the word you want to replace it with in the **Replace with** box. Then select **Replace** or **Replace All**.

18

Figure 18.3
The Browser Objects menu.

Timesaver tip

You can also open the **Browser Objects** menu by using the keyboard shortcut **Alt+Ctrl+Home**.

Find and Replace comes in handy when you want to replace a single word and even a phrase, but what if you want to replace a sentence or a paragraph? To replace a sentence or paragraph, follow these steps:

1 Highlight the text you would like to replace.

2 Press the **Delete** key on your keyboard – this will delete all of the selected text.

3 **Type** the new text you want to replace it with.

To rearrange text, you can use **Cut** and **Paste** commands, or you can use keyboard shortcuts. To use the **Cut** and **Paste** commands:

1 Highlight the text you would like to rearrange, as shown in Figure 18.4.

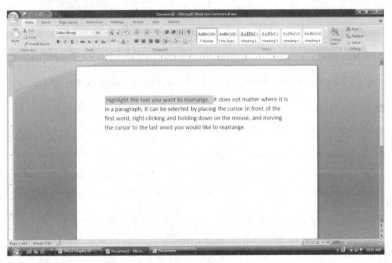

Figure 18.4
Highlight the text to be replaced.

2 On the **Clipboard** section of the **Home** tab, click **Cut**. The text is cut from the page.

3 Place your cursor where you want to insert the text and select **Paste**, as shown in Figure 18.5. The text you cut appears in the area where you have placed your cursor.

18

Figure 18.5
Replace menu.

You can also use keyboard shortcuts to copy and paste:

■ To copy, highlight the text you want copied, then press the **Ctrl+C** keys at the same time.

■ To paste the text, place your cursor where you would like the text to appear and press the **Ctrl+V** keys at the same time. The text you copied appears in the area where you placed your cursor.

One final way to move text in your document is to highlight it, then click and drag it to the new position in the document where you would like it to appear. This is probably the easiest of the options if you're just rearranging text.

→ Using the Clipboard

Every time you use a Cut and Paste or Copy and Paste command, Office 2007 stores the items you have cut or copied on the Office Clipboard, shown in Figure 18.6. You can place up to 24 items at one time on the Clipboard. They remain there until you close out of Microsoft Word. This allows you to go to the Clipboard and retrieve these items if you need them again while you are in Word.

Figure 18.6
Office Clipboard.

To use the Office Clipboard to retrieve an item and insert it into a document, take the following steps:

1 From the Home tab in the Ribbon, click the **Clipboard** menu.

2 Place the cursor in the document where you would like to place an item from the Clipboard.

3 Click the desired Clipboard item to insert it at the point of your cursor in your document.

18

→ Navigating Your Document

The scroll bar to the right of the Word window allows you to scroll through your document in page order.

There are six parts to the scroll bar that allow navigation:

■ Up arrow: Located at the top of the scroll bar, this arrow will move through the document about a line at a time.

■ Down arrow: Located close to the bottom of the scroll bar, this arrow moves you down through a document about a line at a time.

■ Scroll bar: By clicking and holding the scroll bar, you can quickly navigate up and down through the document. You can also click anywhere within the scroll bar to move through a document in small jumps.

■ Double up arrow: This takes you to the previous page of your document.

■ Radio button: The Radio button below the double up arrow opens the **Browser Objects** menu from which you can select the **Go To** command.

■ Double down arrow: This arrow takes you to the next page in your document.

Timesaver tip

You can also navigate through your document by using the arrow keys on your keyboard.

Another feature that can be used to navigate your document is the **Go To** command. If you know the specific page number that you would like to view, the **Go To** command will take you right to it.

1 From the **Home** tab on the Ribbon, select the down-pointing arrow next to **Find** (in the **Editing** section).

2 Select **Go To**.

3 In the **Find and Replace** dialogue box that appears, shown in Figure 18.7, select the object to which you would like to go. Then type the specific element in the text box provided. For example, if you choose to go to a page, type the page number. If you choose to go to a comment, type the reviewer's name.

4 Click **Go To**.

Figure 18.7
Go To menu.

Timesaver tip

The **Go To** dialogue box can also be accessed through the **Browser Objects** menu. The Arrow button represents the Go To command.

18

→ Selecting Text

When selecting text, you can select one word or a whole paragraph. To select one word, position your cursor in front of the desired word and double-click your mouse. This will highlight the word, then you can perform whatever action you need. You can triple-click the mouse to select an entire paragraph.

Another way to select more than one word, a sentence or a paragraph is to place your cursor in front of the first word and click and drag the cursor over the text that you would like to highlight.

You can also select all of the text in an entire document by following these steps:

1 From the **Home** tab of the Ribbon, click **Select** (located in the Editing section).

2 Click **Select All**. All of the text and objects in your document are highlighted.

Timesaver tip

Another way to select all of the text and objects in your document is to use the keyboard shortcut **Ctrl+A**.

→ Deleting Text

To delete text, you can **highlight** any text you want to delete and press the **delete** key on your keyboard. You can also place your cursor in front of the word or first word of a group of words and press and hold the **delete** key until all words are deleted. If you are at the end of a sentence or word that you want to delete, you can press the **backspace** key until the text you want deleted is gone.

→ Moving Text Between Documents

With Office 2007, you can move text between documents or copy an entire document into another document. Use the following steps to copy text to another document:

1 Highlight the text or object.

2 Press **Ctrl+C** or choose the **Copy** command from the Clipboard options – your text is copied to the Clipboard.

3 Minimise the document you are copying from.

4 Open the document you are copying to and place your cursor where you would like the object or text to appear.

5 Press **Ctrl+V** or choose the **Paste** command from the Clipboard options – your text or object will appear in the selected position.

You can also move text from one document to another by highlighting the text, click and hold highlighted text, and then drag it to the desired document. To access the desired document, drag the text to the document title on the task bar. This opens the other document, where you can drop the text where desired. The text is completely removed from the original document.

18

19

Adding Visual Appeal to Your Documents

In this lesson you'll learn about fonts and styles.

→ Working with Fonts

When you are working in the Office 2007 Word program, there are many ways you can add visual appeal to your documents to make them look more professional or more exciting. One of these ways is by changing the style, size and appearance of the fonts used in the document. Changing fonts in Word is simple and you can even see a Live Preview of different fonts before you commit to a change.

Selecting Fonts

The Font menu is located on the **Home** tab of the Ribbon, as shown in Figure 19.1.

Figure 19.1
Font commands are in the Home tab of the Word ribbon.

If you click on the arrow box at the right corner of the **Font** title bar, the **Font** dialogue box appears, as shown in Figure 19.2.

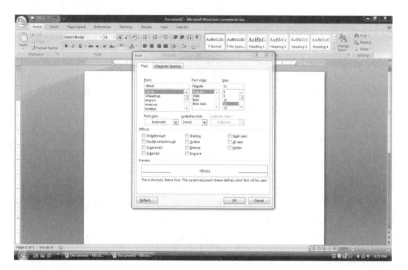

Figure 19.2
Font menu.

The Font dialogue box gives you many choices of actions you can take:

■ **Font**: This is where you select the font style you would like to use in your document.

■ **Font Style**: Choose special formatting for text: italics, bold or other special formatting.

■ **Size**: Choose the size of your text, from 8 points up to 72 points.

■ **Font Color**: Select the colour of your text.

19

- **Underline Style**: Use this command if you want your text to be underlined. It allows you to choose the style of underlining you would like to use.

- **Underline Color**: Select the colour of the line under the text if you choose an underline style.

- **Effects**: Allows you to use effects such as strikethrough or subscript.

The Preview box at the bottom of the menu allows you to preview your choices as you make them to see whether those are the fonts and styles that will work for your document. If you do not like the changes, click the default button to reset the font and styles to the default settings.

If you are happy with the changes, click **OK** to apply the changes and close the menu box.

You can also make the same changes that you make from the Font dialogue box from the Home tab in the Word Ribbon. There is even a highlighting option that allows you to highlight sections of your document, just as you would with paper and a highlighter. The following are commands in the Font section of the Home tab:

- The long drop-down menu at the top of the Font menu is for font selection. Here you will find a list of fonts available to use in your document.

- The drop-down menu next to the Font menu is the Font Size menu.

- The box with the large A and an upward arrow is to incrementally increase your font size.

- The box with the smaller A is to incrementally decrease your font size.

- The icon with the AB and eraser is to clear any formatting in your document and keep the default text.

- The B icon is to select bold formatting.

- The *I* icon is to choose italicised formatting.

- The U with the underline is to choose underlined formatting.

- The button that shows the ABC with a strikethrough allows you to strike through text.

- The button with the X and the subscript 2 is to insert subscript (or lettering that is slightly below the standard lettering).

- The button with an X and a superscript 2 is to insert superscript (or lettering that is slightly above standard lettering).

- The Aa button allows you to change cases, for example from UPPERCASE letters to lowercase letters. There is also a drop-down menu behind this icon that allows you to choose less common cases such as sentence case and tOGGLE cASE.

- The highlighted ab icon is to highlight text.

- The A icon with a red line under it is to choose the colour of your font.

If you want to change the font of an entire document, it is much easier to use the Font dialogue box. However, if you are using special formatting in smaller sections of your document, then highlight the text you want to change and use the **Font** section of the Home tab.

Important

One of the cooler new features of Word 2007 is the floating toolbar. To access this toolbar, highlight a section of text in your document. You'll see the toolbar appear, very transparently, near the highlighted text. To access the toolbar, which contains text formatting commands, move your pointer towards it. If you move your pointer away, the toolbar disappears and won't reappear until you make another text selection.

19

Changing Fonts

To change any font in your document, highlight the text and click the Font drop-down menu on the Font section of the Home tab, as shown in Figure 19.3.

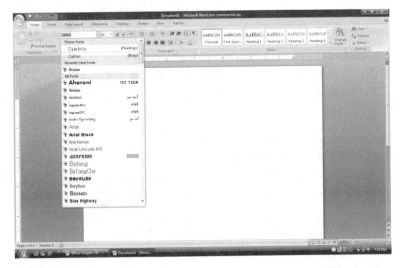

Figure 19.3
Font menu choices.

Browse through the fonts to select the one you would like to use for the document you are creating.

If you want to format an entire document in a different font (the default is Calibri 11), then change the font before you begin typing.

You can change your font size in the same way (before adding text or by highlighting existing text). The Font Size menu is shown in Figure 19.4.

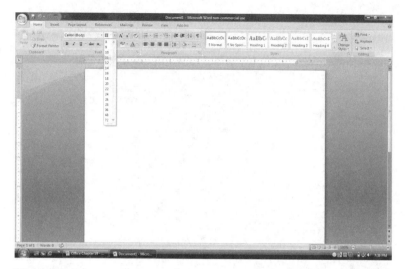

Figure 19.4
The Font Size menu.

→ Working with Styles

Like fonts, you can change the style of your Word document to give more visual appeal. A style is a formatting group that includes fonts, font sizes and even colours for body text, headings, titles and other textual elements of a document. The Styles section is located on the Home tab. If you click the arrow in the far right corner of the Styles commands box, it will bring up the Styles task pane, as shown in Figure 19.5.

By letting your cursor hover over each selection, you can see a description of what that selection is and what it does. Towards the bottom of the menu there are two checkboxes, one of which says Show Preview. By clicking on this box, you can see a preview of what each selection would look like (within the Styles task pane). You can also change text styles using the **Styles** menu on the Ribbon. Click the down-pointing arrow with a line under it on the Styles menu to see a full view of available styles, as shown in Figure 19.6.

19

Figure 19.5
Styles menu.

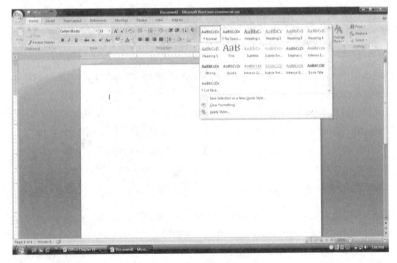

Figure 19.6
Style selection menu.

If you place your cursor in the body of a paragraph and place your pointer over one of the styles in the menu, you can see a Live Preview of what that paragraph would look like in the selected style. To preview a different style, just move your pointer. When you find a style that you would like to use, click the style box and the preview is made permanent.

Next to the text boxes is an icon that says Change Styles. The Change Styles drop-down menu, shown in Figure 19.7, lets you select from predesigned groups of styles to use in your document.

Figure 19.7
Change Styles menu.

There are four different menu options in the Change Styles menu:

1. **Style Set**: When you select Style Select, the Style Set menu appears, as shown in Figure 19.8. You can place your pointer over a style set to preview how it would look in your document. To make the selection permanent, click the selection.

2. **Colors**: The Colors menu shown in Figure 19.9 allows you to choose or create a colour scheme.

19

Figure 19.8
Style Set menu.

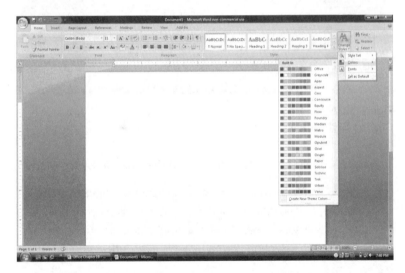

Figure 19.9
Colors menu.

3 **Fonts**: The Fonts menu shown in Figure 19.10 allows you to change the font throughout your document without changing the theme. Again, by hovering over each font, you can see a preview of what the change will look like.

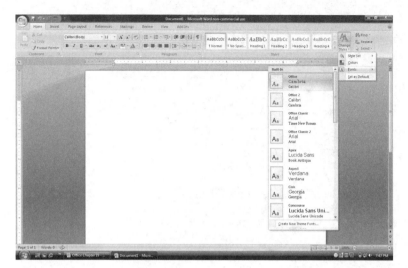

Figure 19.10
Fonts menu.

4 **Set as Default**: Once you make any changes to your style,
you can save those changes as the default setting. Use
caution when selecting this option as it changes the default
font, theme and style for all of the documents that you create
in Word.

Creating and Saving Styles

You can create styles that you use on a regular basis and save
them in Quick Styles to be able to use them for future documents.
Follow these steps to create a custom style:

1 Click the arrow in the bottom right-hand corner of the **Styles**
section on the **Home** tab.

2 At the bottom of the **Styles** task pane, select the **New Style**
icon. The Create New Style from Formatting dialogue box,
shown in Figure 19.11, appears.

19

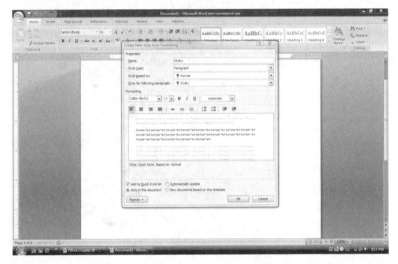

Figure 19.11
Create New Style from Formatting menu.

3 Select the desired options for the new style you are creating. As you are making selections, a preview appears in the preview box.

4 When you've finished designing the style, click **OK** to save your new style and close the window. The style should appear in the **Styles** task pane.

→ Working with Text Alignment

Another option that you have in Word is for text alignment. To access text alignment options, select the **Home** tab and then look for the commands in the **Paragraph** section of the Ribbon, as shown in Figure 19.12.

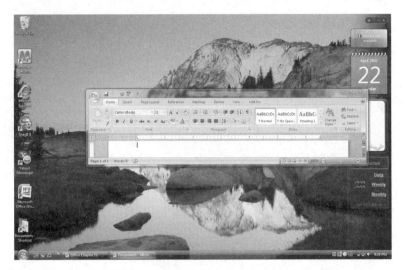

Figure 19.12
Alignment commands.

There are four choices for text alignment, as follows:

1 Left.

2 Middle.

3 Right.

4 Justified.

You can switch back and forth between the alignment commands throughout the document by clicking the command you need. If you have already entered text and would like to change the alignment, you can do so by placing your cursor within a block of text and selecting the correct alignment button.

If you need to change the alignment of the entire document, select all of the text in the document by pressing the **Ctrl+A** keys on your keyboard and then selecting one of the alignment buttons. You can also use keyboard shortcuts instead of clicking an alignment button:

- Align text left: Ctrl+L
- Centre text: Ctrl+E
- Align text right: Ctrl+R
- Justify text: Ctrl+J

20

Using Proofreading Tools

In this lesson you'll learn how to check the spelling and grammar in your documents as well as perform word, page and character counts.

→ Spell Check and AutoCorrect

Two great tools that Office provides in the Word program are Spell Check and AutoCorrect. Spell Check is a tool that will go through your document and check the spelling of the words. If a word is spelled incorrectly, it will show you the word and give you several different spellings to choose from (see Figure 20.1).

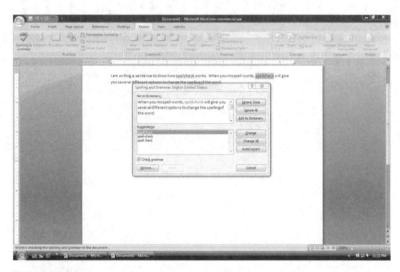

Figure 20.1
Spell Check options.

To use Spell Check, take the following steps:

1 Click the Review tab in the Word Ribbon.

2 From the icons, choose Spelling & Grammar.

Spell Check will check your document for misspelled words and give you the options to correct them.

By default, Office automatically does a spelling and grammar check as you enter text. If the elements of this bother you, such as the coloured squiggly lines, you can turn the spelling and grammar checks off by right-clicking on the book with a pencil over it in the status bar and unchecking the box next to Spelling and Grammar Check.

Office also has an AutoCorrect feature. This has a store of thousands of commonly misspelled words. When you are typing text, if you misspell one of the words in the AutoCorrect library, it will automatically correct itself once you hit the spacebar to begin typing the next word.

→ Proofing as You Type

You can proofread your Word document as you type it to save you having to make all the corrections at once when you do a spelling and grammar check at the end of the document. To do this, place your cursor at the end of a word that has a red or green squiggly line under it and right-click your mouse. This will bring up the menu seen in Figure 20.2.

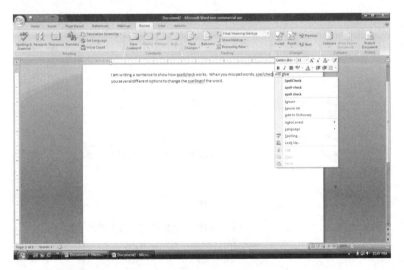

Figure 20.2
Proofing options.

20

Choose the option that will correct the word or group of words. This will correct the mistakes and close the menu.

You can also use the proofreading tool from the status bar. To use the tool from the status bar, take the following steps:

1 Click the proofreading Icon in the status bar (it is the picture of an open book with a pencil hovering over it). A pop-up menu like the one in Figure 20.3 will appear with similar actions as the menu in Figure 20.2.

2 Choose the action you would like to take by clicking it. Depending on the choice you have made, the error will be either ignored or corrected.

Figure 20.3
Proofing menu.

If you let your cursor hover over the proofreading icon for a moment, it will tell you whether there are errors that need correcting before you open the menu (see Figure 20.4).

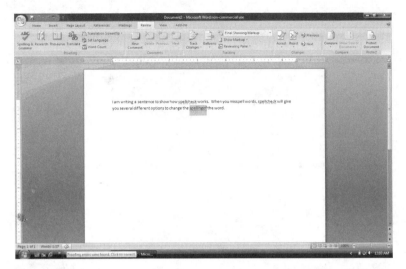

Figure 20.4
Proofing status.

→ Using Grammar Check

Grammar Check works in the same way as Spell Check and Word automatically performs a grammar check when performing a Spell check. As with Spell Check, Office will make suggestions for you to use to correct the grammar error (see Figure 20.5).

There are two ways to use Grammar Check:

1 In the Word Ribbon under the Review tab, click on Spelling & Grammar. This will go through the same process as the Spell Check and will give you options to choose from for grammar errors.

2 Right-click at the end of any group of words underlined in green. A grammar menu will appear. Choose the option that best suits your needs.

You do not have to automatically use the suggestions that Office gives you. You can choose to ignore a suggestion and keep the text the way it is.

20

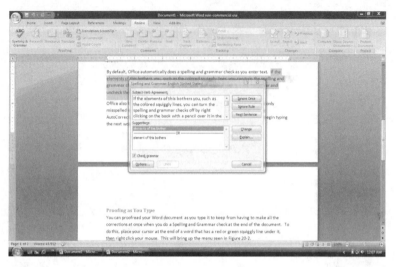

Figure 20.5
Grammar Check suggestion box

→ Using Find and Replace

Find and Replace is a tool that will help you find something you need to rewrite quickly. There are two ways that you can open Find and Replace, one from the Ribbon and one from the slider:

■ Under the Home tab of the Word Ribbon, Find and Replace is found in the last set of commands. To find just a word, click the Find icon. To find and replace a word or group of words, click the Replace icon.

■ At the bottom of the slider bar there are three icons; click the radio button between the two sets of arrows. This will bring up a menu of icons. Click on the binoculars, then choose the Find and Replace tab.

When you use Find and Replace, a box appears (see Figure 20.6) that asks for the word you want to find and the word you want to replace it with. Enter both words and choose from the following options:

1 Replace – this will replace the one word in the section that you searched.

2 Replace All – this will replace that particular word every time it appears in the document.

3 Find Next – if you use Replace to find one word in one place, this will go to the next section of the document and replace the word again.

Once you have completed the Find and Replace task, click the Cancel button to make the window disappear.

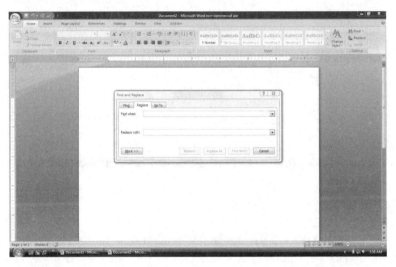

Figure 20.6
Find and Replace.

→ Word Counts, Page Counts and Character Counts

In Word, there is more than one way to check a word or page count. These tools come in handy when you know something has to be a certain length.

20

Located at the right of the toolbar are your page count and word count (see Figure 20.7). As you type your text, the Word counter changes and the page count changes as you add new pages. Be careful of the page count, however. If you make a hard return, your page count may say something like 5 of 6, when actually what you have is five pages of text and a blank page.

Figure 20.7
Page and word counts in toolbar.

You can also get word, page and character counts from the Word Ribbon in the Proofing commands under the Review tab. Take the following steps to receive the counts this way:

1 Click the Review tab on the Ribbon.

2 In the Proofing commands, choose Word Count.

A box similar to the one you see in Figure 20.8 will appear.

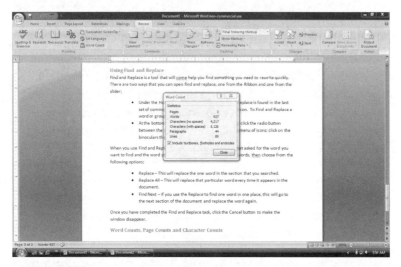

Figure 20.8
Word Count.

This box provides you with the following information:

- **Pages** – how many pages are in your document.

- **Words** – how many words are in your document.

- **Characters (no spaces)** – how many characters are in your documents, without counting the spaces between each one.

- **Characters (with spaces)** – the character count with the spaces being counted also.

- **Paragraphs** – the number of paragraphs in your document.

- **Lines** – the number of lines in your document.

There is also a checkbox that can be checked or unchecked to include text that is in text boxes, footnotes and endnotes. This box is checked by default. If you do not want to include these in the word count, uncheck the box.

→ Using the Thesaurus

Included in the Word program of Office 2007 is the Thesaurus, which contains thousands upon thousands of words. If you have used one word over and over again, or if you feel it just doesn't sound professional enough, you can use the Thesaurus to find another word with the same meaning.

The Thesaurus is located in the Review tab of the Word Ribbon with the Proofing commands. To access the Thesaurus, click on that icon. The Thesaurus will appear in the right corner of your Word window and will look like Figure 20.9.

Figure 20.9
Word Thesaurus.

To use the Thesaurus, type a word in the search box and click the arrow next to it. The results will appear in the box under it. Notice that you can choose the language that you want to search in and that there are back and forward buttons that you can use.

The Thesaurus can be left open in the document window while you finish your document. To close the Thesaurus, click the close button in the top right corner of the Thesaurus window.

→ Using Microsoft's Research Services

Office 2007 has added Research Services to the list of proofing tools at your disposal. The Research options are located as a link at the bottom of the Thesaurus window (see Figure 20.10).

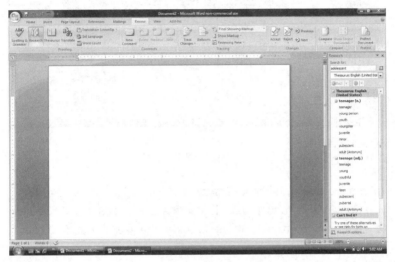

Figure 20.10
Research options command in Thesaurus window.

To open the Research Options, click on the link. When the menu opens, it will look like Figure 20.11.

To use a certain reference in a search, click the box next to that reference choice. Notice that you have access to Research Books, Research Sites and Business and Financial Sites. You will have to have Internet service to utilise some of the reference areas.

You can also Add Services, Update and Remove Services and set Parental Controls from this window. The Parental Controls allows you to set limits on what your child can and cannot view as they are doing a research project on the computer.

20

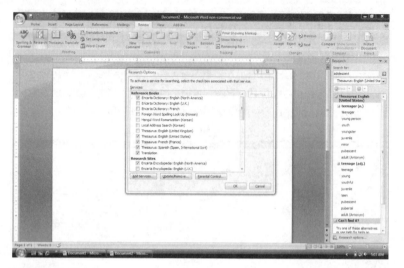

Figure 20.11
Research Options.

To use the research services, type in what you are looking for (as you do with the Thesaurus), choose the references you would like to use from the drop-down menu under the search box and click the green arrow to begin your search.

21

Using AutoFormat

In this lesson you'll be introduced to AutoFormat and learn how to apply it.

→ Understanding AutoFormat

Office 2007 has a tool in Word called AutoFormat that can save loads of time once you are familiar with it and the commands it can perform. AutoFormat automatically formats portions of your document as you create it. There are many options in AutoFormat, including automatic number conversions when you use fractions and automatic entries when you create a bullet or number list.

After you have made your first entry on a bullet or number list and pressed the Enter key on your keyboard, subsequent entries will be set up exactly the same way, in numerical order if you are creating number lists and with bullet points if you're creating a bullet list. This is AutoFormat.

→ Applying AutoFormat

To access the AutoFormat menu and make changes to the commands as needed, take the following steps:

1 Click the **Windows** Button.

2 From the menu that appears, choose **Word Options**. The **Word Options** dialogue box appears.

3 Select **Proofing**.

4 Then select **AutoCorrect Options**; this opens the **AutoCorrect** dialogue box, which has several tabs on it.

5 Choose the **AutoFormat** tab, as shown in Figure 21.1.

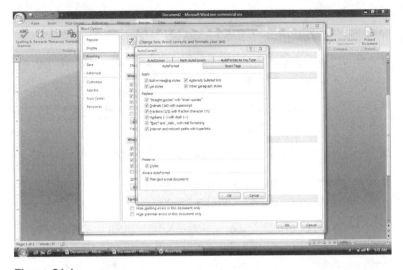

Figure 21.1
AutoFormat.

There is also another AutoFormat tab that reads **AutoFormat As You Type**, as shown in Figure 21.2.

Figure 21.2
AutoFormat As You Type.

The commands that you choose on the AutoFormat tab will apply to entire documents and include the following:

■ **Apply**: This heading includes options such as list styles and automatic bulletted lists.

■ **Replace**: Includes options such as formatting hyphens and bold and italic lettering.

■ **Preserve**: Allows you to preserve styles (selected by default).

■ **Always AutoFormat**: The only option here is plain-text e-mail documents and it is selected by default.

To change AutoFormat options, select or deselect the boxes next to the options you will or will not need when creating a document. Note the default settings in case you are not satisfied with the changes you make.

The AutoFormat As You Type tab gives you the options for the AutoFormat tools that you can use as you add text to your document and is similar in some ways to the AutoFormat tab.

■ **Replace as you type**: Performs the same function as the **Replace as you type** command in AutoFormat options.

■ **Apply as you type**: These are options that you can choose to automatically format certain items as you use them in your document, such as: Automatic bulleted lists, Border lines, Built-in Heading Styles, Automatic numbered lists and tables.

■ **Automatically as you type**: This will automatically apply some of the AutoFormat options as you type in your document, such as formatting the beginning of a list item just like the one before it.

To apply the AutoFormat tools as you are creating a Word document, select the formatting tools that you would like to use, then click **OK** to save the changes and return to your workspace.

22

Using Special Formatting Tools

In this lesson you'll learn about inserting citations, bibliographies, equations and special characters into your documents.

Office 2007 has made it easier to insert information such as footnotes, citations, bibliographies, captions and special characters into your Word documents, saving you both time and frustration. The commands are both quick to learn and quick to use.

→ Inserting Citations

A citation gives credit for information in a document to the source from which that information came. For example, if you reference a journal article or periodical in a document that you're writing, you might want to insert a citation to help readers understand where the information originated. You can find the command to insert citations on the References tab on the Word Ribbon, as shown in Figure 22.1.

Figure 22.1
Insert Citation icon/information.

When inserting citations, you first need a list of sources for Office to use and for you to choose from. You can add items to your source list using the following steps:

1 Click the **References** tab in the Word Ribbon.

2 In the Citations Bibliography commands box, click **Manage Sources**. The **Source Manager** dialogue box, shown in Figure 22.2, appears.

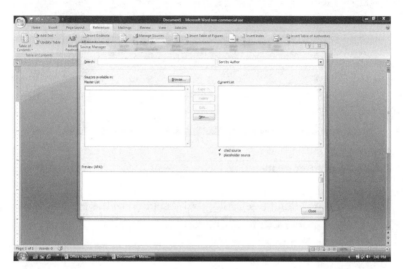

Figure 22.2
Source Manager.

3 Click **New** to open the **Create Source** dialogue box, shown in Figure 22.3.

4 Enter the source information in the text boxes provided and click **OK**.

5 Repeat these steps until your list of sources is complete.

Once you have entered your sources into the Source Manager, you can then insert citations into your document. Take the following actions to insert a citation:

1 Place your cursor at the point in your document where you would like the citation to appear.

2 Select the **References tab** on the Word Ribbon.

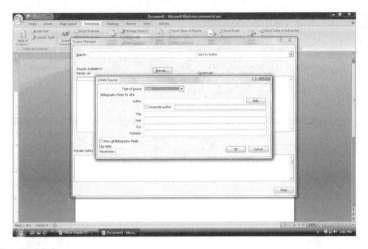

Figure 22.3
Create Source information box.

3 From the Citations & Bibliography section of the Ribbon, choose **Insert Citation**. This opens a drop-down menu, shown in Figure 22.4.

Figure 22.4
Citation menu.

4 Select the source you would like to cite. The citation appears where your cursor is located in your document.

→ Inserting Bibliographies

Remember the sources that you created in the last step when you were citing those references in your documents? Well, once you've cited the references, you'll want to include a bibliography somewhere in your document to display the full information about the sources. You can add bibliographies to your document by following a few simple steps:

1 Place your cursor at the point in your document where you would like the bibliography to appear.

2 Choose the **References** tab on the Word Ribbon.

3 In the Citations & Bibliography section of the Ribbon, select **Bibliography**. This opens a menu of choices for how the bibliography (also called Works Cited) will appear in your document, as shown in Figure 22.5.

Figure 22.5
Bibliography list.

4 Select the format you would like to use and the bibliography appears where your cursor is located in your document.

Using Special Formatting Tools **243**

You can also select the **Insert Bibliography** command to insert your bibliography in your document at the point of your cursor.

→ Using Special Characters and Symbols

You can insert special characters anywhere in any Word document through the Symbols command box. Special characters are those that you cannot access on your keyboard, such as the em dash (—) or the copyright (©) symbol.

The special characters menu is located on Symbol menu on the Insert tab. To insert special characters into your document, do the following:

1 Place your cursor at the point in your document where you want the special character to appear.

2 Go to the **Insert** tab and select **Symbol**. About 20 symbols (or special characters) are displayed in a drop-down menu.

3 If the special character you're seeking isn't in that list, select **More Symbols**. This opens the **Symbol** dialogue box.

4 As shown in Figure 22.6, click the **Special Characters** tab to view the special characters available.

5 Select the desired character, click **Insert** and then click **Close** to return to your document. The special character you have selected should appear in the document at the point of your cursor.

Timesaver tip

Notice that each special character listed has the equivalent keyboard shortcut listed next to it. Make a note of these shortcuts if you use a certain symbol or symbols often as a keyboard shortcut can significantly reduce the amount of time you spend searching for a special character.

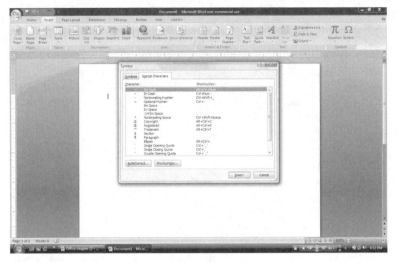

Figure 22.6
Special Characters.

You'll also find there are some AutoCorrect entries for special characters. For example, the copyright symbol can be added to a document by typing (C). Word will automatically change that combination into the copyright symbol: ©.

→ Inserting Equations

You can insert mathematical equations into your Word documents the same way you would insert a special character or symbol. You can also add and save equations for future use. To insert an equation into your document, put the cursor where you would like the equation to appear and take the following steps:

1 Select the **Insert** tab on the Word Ribbon.

2 From the Symbols command box at the end of the Ribbon, click the down arrow under the Equation icon. This opens the Equation drop-down menu, shown in Figure 22.7.

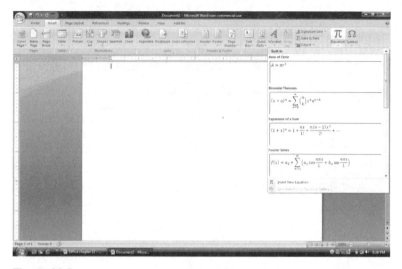

Figure 22.7
Equation menu.

3 Scroll through the menu to select an equation to add to your document.

4 To see more equations and maths symbols, click directly on the **Equation** icon. As shown in Figure 22.8, this opens the **Equation Tools Design** tab and puts a place holder into your document at the point of your cursor where you can type an equation if what you're seeing isn't one of the options on the tab.

5 Select the desired equation and it appears in your document where the placeholder appears.

An easier way to insert a new equation (one that does not already exist in Word) is to click the downward-pointing arrow under the Equation icon and select **Insert New Equation**. An equation box appears in which you can type your new equation.

Once you have entered a new equation, Office will automatically save that equation under the Equation icon for future use.

Figure 22.8
More equations.

23

Adding Graphics to Your Document

In this lesson you'll learn how to insert clip art and pictures into your Word documents. You'll also be introduced to using SmartArt and WordArt.

→ Inserting Clip Art and Pictures

Clip Art and pictures can add interest and appeal to your documents and fortunately, adding these graphic elements to your documents is easy to do.

Clip Art is a ready-to-use graphic file, which can include pictures as well as line drawings and other graphic elements. You'll often see Clip Art and photos as separate types of graphics, however, because of the complexity of using photos in documents. (They're not hard to insert, but do require some special considerations that Clip Art does not – such as file size and resolution depending on whether the picture will be printed or viewed online.)

Both the Clip Art and Picture commands can be found on the Insert tab in the Illustrations section of the Ribbon. To add Clip Art to your document, do the following:

1 Place your cursor in the position in the document where you would like the Clip Art to appear.

2 Go to the **Insert** tab and select **Clip Art**. The Clip Art task pane appears to the right of your document, as shown in Figure 23.1.

3 In the **Search for** text box, enter a keyword or phrase for the type of picture you are looking for.

4 In the drop-down search menu, select the areas of your computer in which you would like to look for the Clip Art.

5 In the drop-down menu for **Results should be**, select the type of media file for which you are searching. You can search for Clip Art, photographs, movies and sounds.

6 Click the **Go** button.

Figure 23.1
Clip Art menu.

7 The search results will appear in the box below your search options. When you find the Clip Art you're searching for, double-click it to insert it in your document at the point of your cursor.

8 Click the X in the top right corner of the Clip Art menu to close it.

Next to the Clip Art icon in the Insert tab is the Picture icon. This is the command you would choose to insert a picture into a Word document. To insert a picture, take the following steps:

1 Place your cursor in the area of the document you would like the picture to appear.

2 Under the **Insert** tab, in the **Illustrations** section, select **Picture**. The **Insert Picture** dialogue box appears, as shown in Figure 23.2.

Figure 23.2
Insert Picture menu.

3 Navigate to and select the picture you would like to insert into your document, then click **Insert**.

4 The picture is placed in your document at the point of your cursor and the **Picture Tools Format** tab is opened, as shown in Figure 23.3.

Important

If you do not have any pictures of your own on your computer, you can insert Microsoft-provided pictures or search for and download publicly licensed pictures on the web. Please use caution when downloading pictures from the web, as they may be copyright protected.

Figure 23.3
Format tab for inserted picture.

→ Adding a Caption

Captions are text descriptions that you insert to explain an object or picture. You can add captions anywhere in a Word document by following these steps:

1 Click the **References** tab on the Ribbon.

2 In the Captions section, select **Insert Caption** to open the **Caption** dialogue box, as shown in Figure 23.4.

3 Under **Caption**, type the caption you would like to use.

4 Under **Options**, choose the type of label you would like: equation, figure or table.

5 Select or deselect the **Exclude label from caption** option.

6 Click **OK**. Your caption appears where your cursor is located in your document.

Figure 23.4
Caption menu.

→ Using SmartArt

SmartArt graphics are advanced graphics such as graphical lists, process diagrams and even more complex graphics. They can be used for a variety of publications, such as business presentations and mathematical papers. Office has a variety of SmartArt that you can insert into a document for a more professional look.

To insert SmartArt into your document, use the following commands:

1 Place your cursor in the area of your document where you would like the SmartArt to appear.

2 In the **Illustrations** section of the **Insert** tab, click the **SmartArt** icon. This opens the **Choose a SmartArt Graphic** dialogue box, shown in Figure 23.5.

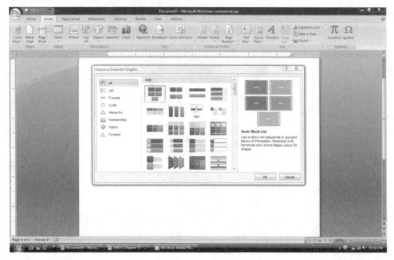

Figure 23.5
The Choose a SmartArt Graphic dialogue box.

3 Select the category of graphic you would like to use.

4 Then select the graphic you would like to insert and click **OK**. It appears in your document at the point of your cursor.

5 Now you can type the text that you would like to have included in the SmartArt in the spaces provided, as shown in Figure 23.6.

6 Once you have finished entering text you can further customise your SmartArt by changing the design colours and borders using the tools provided in the **SmartArt Tools Design** tab, shown in Figure 23.7.

7 When you've finished working with the SmartArt Design, click in any blank space outside the graphic to return to the text structure of your document.

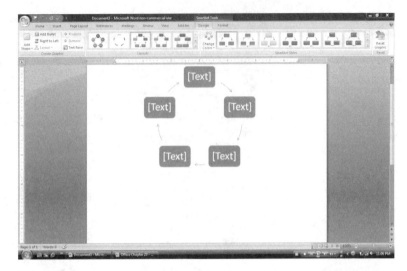

Figure 23.6
Enter text into the SmartArt graphic.

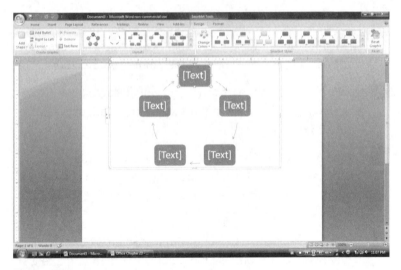

Figure 23.7
Graphic Design menu.

→ Adding Charts

You can add charts to your Word document by choosing the Chart icon in the Illustrations section of the Insert tab. Then take the following steps to insert a chart into your document:

1 Place your cursor at the point in your document where you would like the chart to appear.

2 Click the Chart icon.

3 Select the desired Chart from the **Insert Chart** dialogue box, shown in Figure 23.8.

Figure 23.8
Chart menu.

4 Click OK and the chart appears in the position of your cursor. At the same time, a Microsoft Excel worksheet opens, as shown in Figure 23.9.

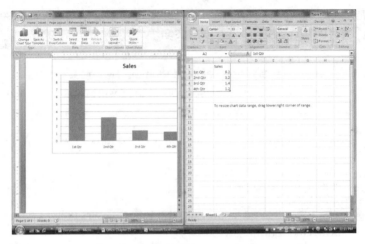

Figure 23.9
Split screen with Word and Excel programs and options.

5 Type the data you would like reflected in the chart into the Excel worksheet and then save it to have that data reflected in the chart.

6 When you've finished entering data for the chart, you can further customise the chart using the Chart Tools Design tab shown in Figure 23.10.

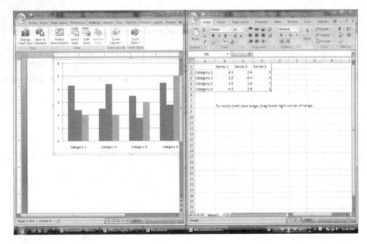

Figure 23.10
Chart editing ribbon.

→ Using WordArt

You can use WordArt to bring a fun visual appeal to your documents by "dressing up" your words.

23

Use these steps to insert WordArt into a document:

1 Place your cursor at the point in the document where you would like the WordArt to appear.

2 In the Text section of the Insert tab, select the WordArt icon. The WordArt menu, shown in Figure 23.11, appears.

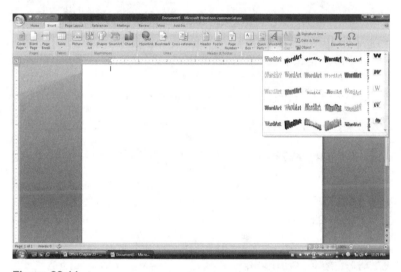

Figure 23.11
WordArt options.

3 Choose the style of WordArt you would like to insert and then the **Edit WordArt Text** dialogue box appears, as shown in Figure 23.12.

Figure 23.12
Edit WordArt Text.

4 Choose font and font size from drop-down menus.

5 If you want bold or italic lettering (or both), click these icons.

6 Type the text you would like to appear as the selected WordArt.

7 Click **OK**. Your text appears in your document, as shown in Figure 23.13.

Once your WordArt appears in the document, you should see the **WordArt Tools Format** tab. This tab appears as long as the WordArt is selected. Using the commands on this tab you can further customise your WordArt.

Figure 23.13
WordArt as it might appear in a document.

24

Using Quick Parts

In this lesson you'll be introduced to Quick Parts and learn how to add them to your documents.

→ Understanding Quick Parts

One very interesting new function in Word 2007 is Quick Parts. Quick Parts are small snippets of formatting or text that you use repeatedly in the documents that you create every day. The Quick Parts option is located on the Text section of the Insert tab on the Ribbon, as shown in Figure 24.1.

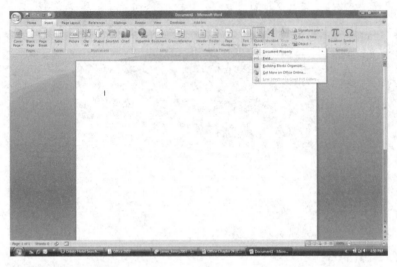

Figure 24.1
The Quick Parts menu.

From the Quick Parts menu you can access the following options:

1 **Document Property**: Lets you insert properties such as Author, Category, Comments, Keywords, Status, Subject and Title.

2 **Field**: Allows you to quickly insert a field into your document. When you select the Field option you're taken to the Field dialogue box, shown in Figure 24.2. In that dialogue box, select the field you want to insert into your document.

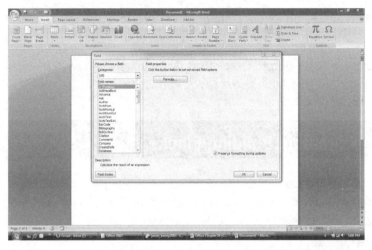

Figure 24.2
Use the Field dialogue box to insert fields into your document.

■ **Building Blocks Organizer**: Lets you manage and edit the
building blocks in the Quick Parts section. As you can see in
Figure 24.3, there's already a considerable list of available
building blocks, but you can edit and add to these according to
your needs as you're creating documents.

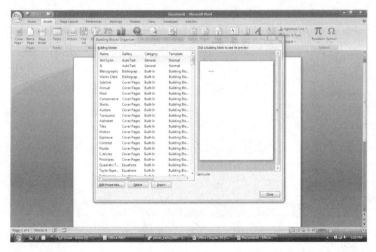

Figure 24.3
The Building Blocks Organizer.

- **Get More on Office Online**: Allows you to download Quick Parts from the Office Online web site.

- **Save Selection to Quick Part Gallery**: Lets you save a block of highlighted text to the Quick Part Gallery for future use.

→ Creating Building Blocks

If you're working in a document that already has sections of text that you would like to use in another document, you can save those sections to the Quick Part Gallery using these steps:

1 Highlight the text you want to add to the gallery.

2 Select the **Insert** tab and then click **Quick Parts**.

3 Select **Save Selection to Quick Part Gallery** from the Quick Parts menu. A **Create New Building Block** dialogue box appears, as shown in Figure 24.4.

Figure 24.4
Create a new building block.

4 Create a name for the building block.

5 Select the gallery in which to store it.

6 Add a description if desired.

7 Then click **Save** and the new building block is added to the gallery.

Then the next time you want to add that text to a document it's only a click away.

→ Adding Quick Parts to Your Document

To add a Quick Part to your document:

1 Place your cursor at the point in your document where you want the Quick Part to appear.

2 Go to **Insert > Quick Parts**.

3 Select **Building Blocks Organizer** and then choose the desired part from the dialogue box that appears.

4 Select **Insert** and the part is added to your document at the point of your cursor.

→ Customising Quick Parts

When you add a Quick Part to your document, you're automatically taken to the **Design** tab for that element, as shown in Figure 24.5.

From this tab, you can change or customise your chosen Quick Part. For example, if the Quick Part you inserted was a table, as in Figure 24.5, you will be taken to the **Table Tools Design** tab, where you can change or customise the table.

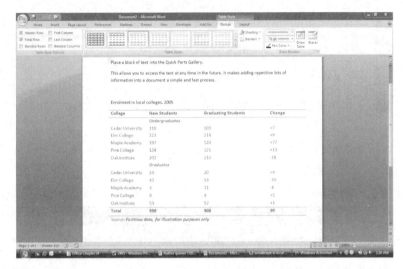

Figure 24.5
Contextual tabs make it easy to customise Quick Parts.

25

Printing Your Documents

In this lesson you'll learn how to change print settings and preview your print jobs before sending them to the printer.

→ Sending Your Documents to the Printer

Once you have finished typing, editing and adding illustrations to your Word document, you may want to print them. Before you do, be sure to save your document to keep from losing all or parts of it in the event of a malfunction or system crash.

To send a document to the printer:

1 Click the **Windows** Button.

2 Highlight **Print** and a Print menu appears.

3 Select Print. The **Print** dialogue box appears, as shown in Figure 25.1.

Figure 25.1
Print menu.

4 Select the printer you want to use.

5 Choose the **Page Range** to print a selection of pages or select all to print all of your document.

6 Choose the number of copies to print.

7 Click OK and your document is sent to the printer.

→ Changing Your Print Settings

In the Print menu (seen in Figure 25.1), there are several different settings that you can change to adjust how your document prints. Here is a brief preview of the Print settings:

- **Name**: Choose the printer you wish to print from listed in the drop-down menu if you have more than one printer.

- **Page range**: Choose to print the entire document, the current page, selected parts, or selected pages.

- **Copies**: Choose how many copies of the document to print.

- **Zoom**: Choose how many pages print on each piece of paper and whether to scale to the size of the paper.

- **Properties**: Click this box to change print quality and to choose a strictly black and white document or choose to print colours if there are different colours in the document.

- **Options**: See Figure 25.2. Displays Word printing options.

→ Previewing Your Print Job

If you want to preview your document to see how it will look once it is printed, you can do so by using the Print Preview command in the Windows Button menu. To see a print preview, do the following:

1 Click the **Windows** Button.

2 Choose the **Print** option – the print options appear (see Figure 25.3).

3 Select Print Preview – this opens a window that will illustrate

25

Figure 25.2
Word printing options.

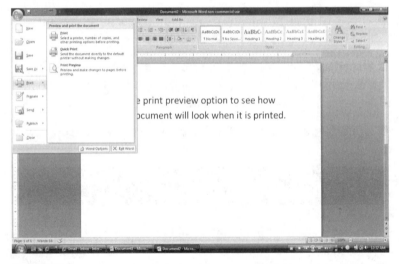

Figure 25.3
Print options.

how your document will appear when it is printed (see Figure 25.4).

4 To exit Print Preview, click the **Close Print Preview**.

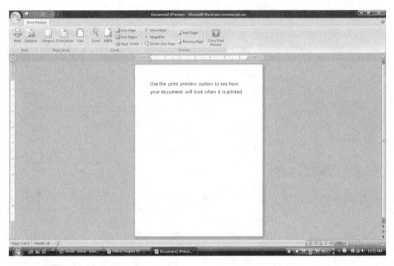

Figure 25.4
Print Preview.

Overview of Excel 2007

26

Getting Started with Excel

In this lesson you'll learn how to open, close and customise Excel and familiarise yourself with Workbooks.

→ Opening Excel

Unless you have a shortcut on your desktop for the Excel
program, it will have to be opened from the Start menu. To open
Excel from the Start menu, do the following:

1 Click the **Windows** Button.

2 Select **All Programs**.

3 Select **Microsoft Office**.

4 Choose **Microsoft Office Excel 2007**. An Excel workbook
appears, as shown in Figure 26.1.

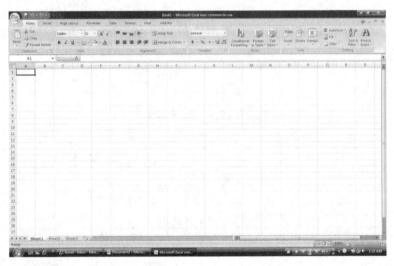

Figure 26.1
Excel workbook.

→ Using the Excel Ribbon

Like all other Office Ribbons, the Excel Ribbon contains
contextual tabs that group similar commands under one tab for
easy access and use (see Figure 26.2).

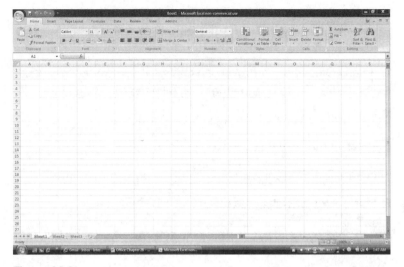

Figure 26.2
Excel Ribbon.

There are eight contextual tabs in the Excel Ribbon. They are:

■ **Home tab**: The Home tab contains the most commonly used commands such as the Clipboard (cut, copy and paste), font and alignment commands.

■ **Insert tab**: This tab contains commands to insert objects such as tables, illustrations and charts.

■ **Page Layout tab**: These commands are used to customise pages and contain commands such as Themes and Page Setup.

■ **Formulas tab**: This tab has commands to customise Excel formulas.

■ **Data tab**: This contains data commands such as Data Connections and Data Tools.

■ **Review tab**: The Review tab contains commands such as Spell Check and Changes.

■ **View**: This contains commands for workbook views and window views.

■ **Add-Ins**: The Add-Ins tab is where you manage program add-ins.

→ Changing Your View

As in any Office program, you can change the way you view your Excel workbook. To change the view, take the following steps:

1 Select the **View** tab from the Excel Ribbon.

2 Select the view that you would like to use.

There are five different ways you can view an Excel workbook:

■ **Normal View**: This is the default view (see Figure 26.3).

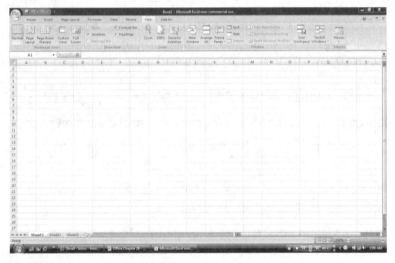

Figure 26.3
Normal View.

■ **Page Layout View**: Allows you to view the workbook as it would look on a printed page (see Figure 26.4).

■ **Page Break Preview**: Allows you to see where the page breaks will be when the workbook is printed.

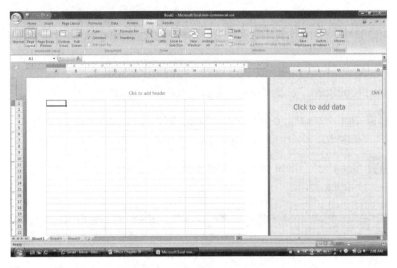

Figure 26.4
Page Layout View.

■ **Custom View**: Allows you to save a set of display and print settings for a custom view.

■ **Full Screen View**: Allows a full screen view of the workbook for easier viewing (see Figure 26.5).

Figure 26.5
Full Screen View.

→ Customising Excel

You can customise the features of Excel to modify how it looks and functions. To customise Excel, follow these steps:

1 Open the Microsoft Office Excel 2007 program from the desktop shortcut or Windows button.

2 Click the Office Button and a menu appears, as shown in Figure 26.6.

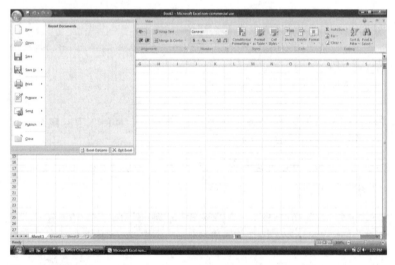

Figure 26.6
Excel Office button pull-down menu.

3 Select the **Excel Options** button in the bottom right corner of the menu. The **Options** dialogue box appears (see Figure 26.7).

4 Select a category to make changes in.

5 Choose the changes you would like to make.

6 Click **OK** to save your changes and exit the **Options** dialogue box.

Figure 26.7
Excel Options menu.

Important

Each category in the Excel Options menu has a brief explanation of
what can be customised under that category. However, customising
Excel is much the same as customising Word.

→ Starting and Opening Workbooks

Once you have become familiar with the Excel Ribbon and other
options that the program offers, you can open and start working
in an Excel workbook. A workbook is an Excel file that you are
working in or have saved, just like you have documents in Word.

To open a new workbook, simply open the Excel program. A
blank workbook will appear, as shown in Figure 26.8.

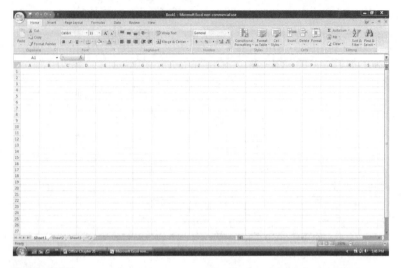

Figure 26.8
New, blank Excel workbook.

To begin working in a new workbook in Excel, click on a cell and start entering information.

To open an existing workbook, take the following steps:

1 Open the Excel program.

2 Click the Windows button.

3 Select **Open** from the menu that appears. This opens the **Open** dialogue box, shown in Figure 26.9.

4 Navigate to and select the file to open and click the **Open** button.

You can also open recent workbooks from the right side of the pull-down menu that appears when you click the Windows button. Just double-click the workbook you would like to open.

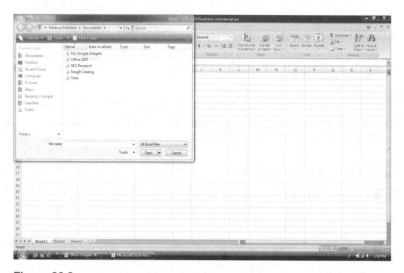

Figure 26.9
File Menu.

→ Saving and Closing Workbooks

It is always a good idea to save your work every few minutes to keep from losing it unexpectedly. As with saving in Word, you can use the keyboard shortcut **Ctrl+S**. The first time you do this, you will be prompted to name your workbook and select a location to which you would like it saved. After the first time, using the keyboard shortcut will simply save your progress.

When you have finished with a workbook and are ready to save and close the workbook, you can use the same shortcut as above to save the workbook or you can take the following steps:

1 Click the Windows button.

2 Select **Save As** and choose the format and location you would like to save the workbook in.

3 Name the workbook.

4 Click **Save**. Then close out of the workbook by clicking the **X** in the upper right corner.

Another option for saving your workbook is to click on the Save icon in the Quick Access Toolbar. Again, the first time you save a workbook, you will be prompted to name it and select a location to which you wish it saved.

Once you have saved your workbook, you can close the current Excel window and open a new workbook. To do this, take the following steps:

1 Click the Windows button.

2 Select **Close**. The current workbook disappears.

3 Click the Windows button again.

4 Select **New**. This opens the **New Workbook** dialogue box, shown in Figure 26.10.

Figure 26.10
New document options menu.

5 Select **Blank**, or choose from one of the Excel template categories on the left.

6 Click **Create** and the new workbook appears.

→ Closing Excel

When you have finished working in Excel, you have three options to close the program:

- Click the **X** in the top right corner of the workbook.

- Click the Windows button and choose **Exit Excel**.

- Use the keyboard shortcut **Ctrl+X**.

Remember to save your workbooks before exiting out of the Microsoft Office Excel 2007 program.

26

27

Working with Data

In this lesson you'll learn about Data Types including how to enter data, text, numbers, dates and times. You'll also learn how to use the AutoFill Function.

→ Understanding Data Types

When working in Excel, you need to know and understand what data makes up a spreadsheet or workbook. There are three major data types used in the Excel 2007 program:

- numbers
- text (labels)
- formulas.

Each one of these is considered a type of data and all hold important positions in the Excel 2007 program.

→ Entering Data

You can enter any type of data into an Excel spreadsheet by clicking on the cell you want to enter data into and then typing the data. However, Office gives you a plethora of ways to format the data that you use.

Entering Text

You can format text in an Excel spreadsheet from the Font section on the Home tab of the Excel Ribbon (see Figure 27.1).

Excel gives you the following formatting choices in the Font commands box:

- **Font Box**: Click the downward arrow to choose a font face.
- **Font Size**: Click the downward arrow to choose font size.
- **Large A icon**: Increase font size.
- **Small A icon**: Decrease font size.
- **B**: Click to use bold lettering.

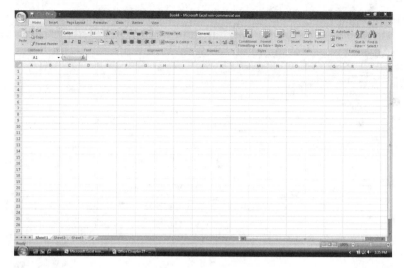

Figure 27.1
Font menu.

■ **I**: Click to use italicised lettering.

■ **U**: Click to underline text.

■ **Add Bottom Border**: Click here to add a bottom border to your spreadsheet.

■ **Use Fill Color**: Click here to use Fill Color.

■ **Choose Font Color**: Choose the colour you would like data to appear as.

Use any of these options to format your text for a more professional appeal.

Entering Numbers

You can format numbers in cells by selecting the cell and using the commands in the **Number** section of the **Home** tab, shown in Figure 27.2.

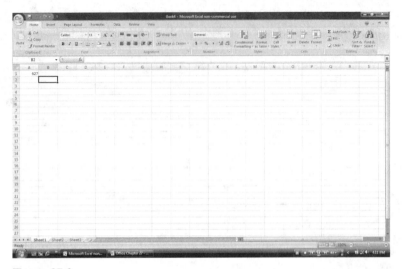

Figure 27.2
Number options.

For more options, you can click the small box to the bottom right corner of the **Number** section. This opens up the **Format** dialogue box, shown in Figure 27.3.

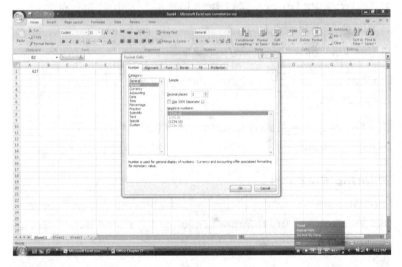

Figure 27.3
Format Cells menu.

Click the **Number** tab for format options. You can view samples of the formats by clicking on each category. A description of each selection appears under the sample window.

To change the Number format from this menu, do the following:

1 Select the **Format** option that you want to use.

2 Make changes using the format menu in the right of the option screen.

3 Click **OK** to save the format changes and close the Format menu.

Entering Dates and Times

Formatting options for dates and times are also located in the **Number** section on the **Home** tab. To format dates and times, follow these steps:

1 In the **Number** section, click the small box in the bottom right corner of the section.

2 In the **Format Cells** dialogue box that appears, choose the **Numbers** tab.

3 Under **Category**, choose **Time or Date** (see Figure 27.4).

4 Choose the type of time or date you would like to use.

5 Choose the language to use.

6 Click **OK** to save your changes and return to your workbook.

→ Copying Data to Other Cells

You can copy data from one cell and enter it into another chosen cell by using keyboard shortcuts or the Copy and Paste commands in the Clipboard.

Figure 27.4
Choose Date or Time from the category to format the date or time.

To copy data using keyboard shortcuts:

1 Highlight the data to copy and press **Ctrl+C**.

2 Select the **cell** to copy the data to.

3 Press **Ctrl+V**. The data appears in the selected cell.

To use the Clipboard commands, do the following:

1 Choose the data to copy.

2 Click the **Copy** command in the Clipboard section of the **Home** tab.

3 Select the cell to copy the data to.

4 Select **Paste** and the data appears in the selected cell.

Using the AutoFill Function

Excel 2007 has an option that keeps you from typing repetitive data. This option finishes text and numbers for you once you start typing them. This option is called AutoFill. To use AutoFill, take the following steps:

1 Click a cell and type the data (such as a month).

2 A box appears in the bottom right corner of the cell. This is called a **Fill Handle**.

3 Move the cursor over the **Fill Handle** until the cursor becomes a cross-hair box.

4 Hold the left mouse button and move the mouse through the cells that you would like the data to appear in: as you do this, the AutoFill will enter the data into the selected cells (see Figure 27.5).

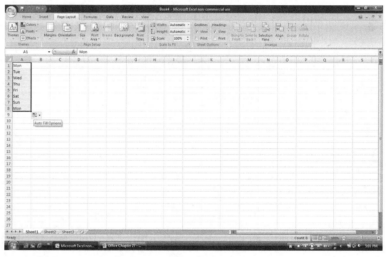

Figure 27.5
Excel uses the AutoFill command to fill in similar cells.

28

Understanding Formulas and Calculations

In this lesson you'll learn about displaying, editing and deleting formulas and working with formula operators. You'll also learn how to use the AutoSum feature.

→ Understanding Formulas

Formulas take data from one cell or a group of cells and use that data to calculate results that appear in another cell. Formulas can be simple, such as adding two numbers together, or very complex, such as calculation of a second-order differential equation.

Using Formula Operators

Formula operators specify the type of calculation you want to perform on the elements of a formula. There are four types of operators: arithmetic, comparison, text concatenation and reference.

The arithmetic operators are used to perform basic maths such as addition, subtraction and multiplication. The following are arithmetic operators:

- **plus sign** (+) – used for addition: example 2+2

- **minus sign** (-) – used for subtraction: example 2–2

- **asterisk** (*) – used for multiplication: example 2*2

- **forward slash** (/) – used for division: example 2/2

- **percent** (%) – used for percentage: example 50%

- **caret** (^) – used for exponentiation: example 2^2

The comparison operators are used to compare two values. The following are comparison operators:

- **equals sign** (=) – equal to: example 2=2

- **greater than sign** (>) – greater than: example 2>1

- **less than sign** (<) – less than: example 1<2

- **greater than or equal to sign** (>=) – greater than or equal to: example 2>=2

- **not equal to sign** (<>) – not equal to: example 2<>1

There is only one text concatenation operator. This is used to join, or concatenate, two values to produce a single continuous value.

■ **ampersand** (&) – used to join two values to produce one: example "South" & "West" & "Wind" = SouthWestWind

The reference operators combine ranges of cells for calculations. The following are reference operators:

■ **Colon** (:) – produces one reference to all cells between two references, to include the two references: example A2:A12

■ **Comma** (,) combines multiple references into one: example SUM (A6:A2,A12:A8)

■ **Space** – produces one reference to cells common to two references.

Understanding Order of Operations

When several operators are used in a single formula, Excel follows a predetermined order of operations. The following is the order the operators are used in:

1 : (colon)

2 (single space)

3 , (comma)

    – (negation)

4 % (percent)

5 ^ (exponentiation)

6 and / (multiplication and division)

7 + and – (addition and subtraction)

8 &

9 =

10 < >

11 <=

12 >=

13 <>

The order of operations is not set in stone and it can be changed. To change the order of operation, enclose the part of the formula that you would calculate first in parentheses. For example: with =5–4*12 the answer would be 43 with the normal order of operations. By using parentheses in the formula, however, (=(5–4)*12) the answer will be 12.

→ Entering Formulas in Cells

To automatically calculate anything in Excel, you must use a formula. A formula consists of the equals sign (=), at least two cell references (A,B) and one or more formula operators. These formulas must be entered into a cell to automatically perform its function. Here is an example of a formula:

=A2+B2+C2+D2

Use the following steps to enter a formula into a cell:

1 Select the cell where you would like to use the formula: the cell will be highlighted.

2 Enter the equals sign (=) into the cell.

3 Type your formula using at least two cell references that contain data and the formula operators.

4 Press Enter.

Figure 28.1 is an example of how your formula should look on your spreadsheet.

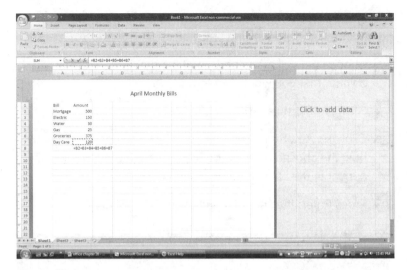

Figure 28.1
Enter your formula into a cell.

Timesaver tip

As you type, notice that your formula appears in the formula bar above the spreadsheet. Instead of pressing Enter to insert your formula, you can click the checkmark in the toolbar and it will enter the formula in that cell.

Entering cell numbers can become an aggravating and repetitive task. To make it easier, use your mouse to click each cell that you would like to include in the formula. You will still have to type in the operators.

→ Using the AutoSum Feature

When you want to add together two or more cells in a row or column but want to avoid the aggravation of entering the formula to do so, you can use the AutoSum command. AutoSum is a useful command that uses the SUM function to keep you from typing in the cell references for a formula. To use the AutoSum command, take the following steps:

1 Choose the cell at the bottom of the row or right of the column that you would like to add.

2 Click the Formula tab.

3 Click the AutoSum icon in the Function Library commands box: the chosen cells will be highlighted and a formula will appear in the chosen cell (see Figure 28.2).

4 Press Enter: the sum of the chosen cells will appear.

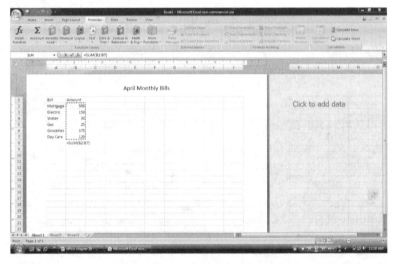

Figure 28.2
Using the AutoSum feature.

→ Displaying, Editing and Deleting Formulas

There will come a time when you want to view, edit or delete formulas that you are using. You can display a formula in the Formula bar or in the cell itself. To view a formula in the Formula bar, simply choose the cell the formula is used in. It will appear in the Formula bar when you select the cell. To view a formula in the cell that it is used in, double-click that cell.

Once created, formulas can be edited at any time. You can edit formulas in the Formula bar or in the cell itself. To edit a formula from the Formula bar:

1 Select the cell that contains the formula.

2 Click on the Formula bar and edit your formula (see Figure 28.3).

3 Click Enter to apply and save the new formula.

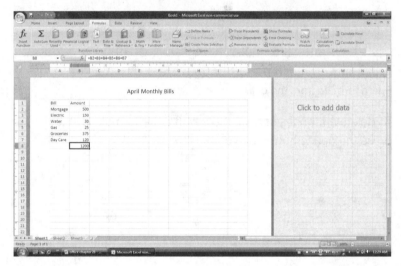

Figure 28.3
Use the Formula bar to edit a formula.

To edit a formula from the cell itself:

1 Double-click the cell that contains the formula: the formula will appear (see Figure 28.4).

2 Edit the formula.

3 Click Enter to apply and save the new formula.

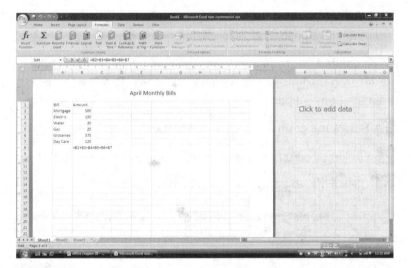

Figure 28.4
Edit a formula from the cell.

To delete a formula, choose the cell that the formula is in and press the delete button on your keyboard.

29

Working with Graphs and Charts

In this lesson you'll learn how to add, edit and delete graphs and charts.

→ Understanding Graphs and Charts

There are times when using charts in Excel spreadsheets is a must. Before using charts, however, you need to have at least a basic understanding of the parts of a chart and what their purpose is.

There are five parts to most charts that you will use in Excel. These are:

■ **chart title**: The title explains what the chart is for.

■ **data series**: The data series is the numeric data used for creating a chart.

■ **X axis**: The width of the chart.

■ **Y axis**: The height of the chart.

■ **legend**: Explains what each part of the chart means.

Excel 2007 contains a large variety of charts that can be inserted into a spreadsheet. The four most popular are the pie chart, column chart, line chart and bar chart:

■ **Pie chart**: Used to display the contribution of each value to a total: see Figure 29.1.

■ **Column chart**: Used to compare values across categories: see Figure 29.2.

■ **Line chart**: Used to display trends over time: see Figure 29.3.

■ **Bar chart**: Used to compare multiple values: see Figure 29.4.

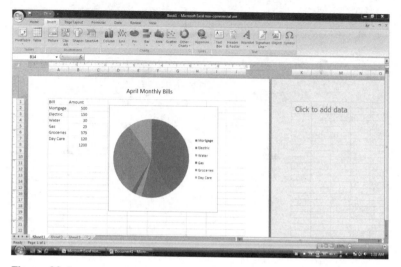

Figure 29.1
Pie chart.

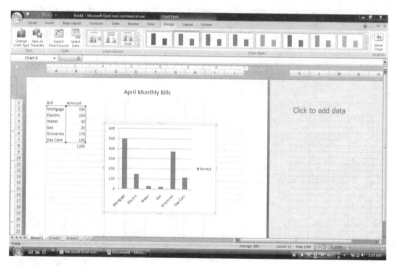

Figure 29.2
Column chart.

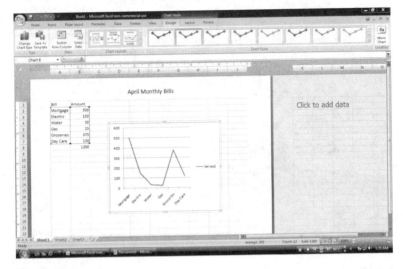

Figure 29.3
Line chart.

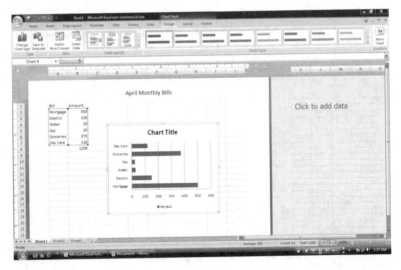

Figure 29.4
Bar chart

→ Adding Graphs and Charts

To create a chart you will need to already have data in your Excel spreadsheet. Keep in mind that a chart can be edited at any time, so if you decide you do not like the information it contains, it can be changed.

To create a chart, take the following steps:

1 Select the data you would like to appear in the chart: you must have both numbers and labels to create the chart.

2 Click the **Insert** tab in the Excel Ribbon: the Charts group is under this tab (see Figure 29.5).

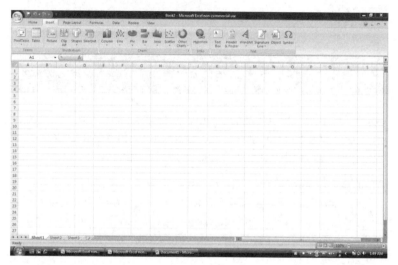

Figure 29.5
Charts.

3 Click the icon of the type of chart you would like to insert: a chart gallery will appear.

4 Choose the chart you want to insert: a chart will appear in your spreadsheet, along with a design tab (see Figure 29.6).

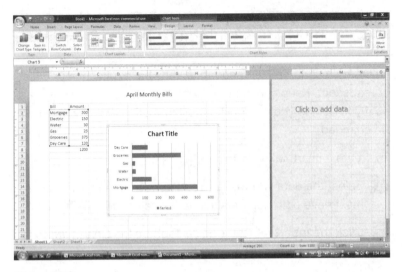

Figure 29.6
Design tab.

→ Editing Graphs and Charts

Once you insert an Excel chart into a spreadsheet you can, at any time, go back and edit the chart. Charts can be moved, resized or changed completely by using the Chart Design tab.

When you create a chart, Excel puts it in just any old place in your spreadsheet, and most of the time that means over data that has already been entered. The chart can be moved to a different part of the spreadsheet. To move a chart to a different area of a spreadsheet, do the following:

1 Move the cursor over the edges of the chart until it (the cursor) turns into a four-way pointer.

2 Hold down the left mouse button and drag the mouse to move the chart.

3 When the chart is in the area you would like it to appear, release the mouse: the chart will appear in that spot.

Not only can a chart be moved, it can also be resized. To resize a chart, take the following steps:

1 Move the cursor over the corners or mid-sides of the chart until the cursor turns into a two-way pointer.

2 Hold down the left mouse button and move the pointer until the sides or corners are where you would like them to be.

3 Release the mouse button when you are satisfied with the size of the chart.

You can also use the Chart Design tab to edit your chart. The Chart Design tab appears when you create a chart or when you click on an existing chart. There are five categories to choose from when changing the design of your chart:

■ **Type**: Lets you change the chart type or save the current chart as a template.

■ **Data**: Lets you change the source from which the chart gets its data.

■ **Chart Layout**: Allows you to change each individual element of the chart, such as the title or the legend.

■ **Chart Styles**: Gives you several different choices to change the appearance of the chart.

■ **Location**: Gives the option to move the chart to another sheet or tab in the Excel workbook.

→ Deleting Graphs and Charts

You may decide that a chart you inserted into your spreadsheet or workbook is not what you expected it to be in appearance or impact. In this situation, the chart can be deleted. To delete a chart, simply click on the chart and hit the delete button on your keyboard. The chart will disappear.

29

If, once you delete the chart, you immediately decide you should have left it in the spreadsheet, simply click the back button in the Quick Access Toolbar and the chart will reappear. This works only until you enter more data. If you try it after that, you will lose the data that you entered after deleting the chart.

30

Editing Excel Spreadsheets

In this lesson you'll learn about correcting, copying, moving and deleting data.

→ Correcting Data

We all know too well that none of us is perfect, although at times we would like to think we are. Formulas in Excel and the results they give us depend completely on whether we enter our data correctly. It is always a good idea to recheck the answers that Excel formulas give you for a given series of numbers. If you find that the formula answer is not correct, you will need to double check the data and the formula used for calculating it.

If you find that you have input incorrect data, you can click on the cell that holds the data and change it to the correct entry. Once you select a cell and start typing, the previous data will disappear.

If you find that the data is correct, you need to look at the formula and test it to make sure that it is entered correctly. For example, if you intend to add together two numbers, such as 5+5 which equals 10, but you are getting the answer 25, you know that you are multiplying the figures by mistake. Simply change your operators in the formula.

→ Undoing an Action

The great thing about any Office 2007 program you may be working in is that they all have an undo icon located in the Quick Access Toolbar. The Quick Access Toolbar is to the right of the Office Button (unless you chose to move it somewhere else).

If you have taken an action and are not happy with the results of that action, such as adding a chart or trying to fix a formula unsuccessfully, simply click the undo arrow in the Quick Access Toolbar. The spreadsheet will return to the previous state that it was in, losing any data or object that was added before you hit the undo arrow.

If you undo something you have done and you want it back, click the forward button in the Quick Access Toolbar and Excel will retrieve the action for you.

Keep in mind that the undo and redo actions will work only immediately after entering data or undoing the action. Once you have moved on, to get back to the action you would like to undo by using the undo button you will lose every bit of data that has been input from that point.

→ Using the Replace Feature

Like the Word program, Excel has a Find and Replace feature (see Figure 30.1).

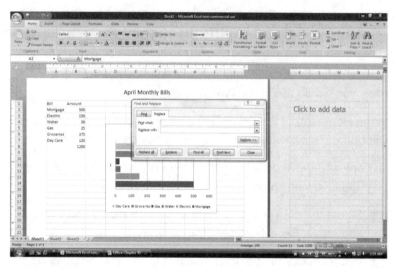

Figure 30.1
Find and Replace.

This tool comes in handy if you know what you are looking for and what you would like to replace it with. To use the Find and Replace feature, do the following:

1 In the Editing group under the Home tab, select the **Find & Select** icon.

2 Choose **Replace** from the drop-down menu that appears: this will bring up the Find and Replace menu.

3 In the **Find what** box, type in what you would like to find.

4 In the **Replace with** box, type in what you would like to replace it with.

5 Choose to **Replace All**, which will replace all instances of the item you selected, or choose **Replace**, which will replace only what you have selected in the area you are in. If you would like to replace the next instance of the same selection, click **Find Next**.

→ Copying and Moving Data

You can copy and move data in Excel with the same Clipboard tools you would use in the Word program.

In the Home tab of the Excel Ribbon there is a category called Clipboard. This is where your copy commands are located.

To copy and move data from one cell or group of cells to another, take the following steps:

1 Select the data or group of data that you would like to copy and move: Excel highlights the cells.

2 In the Clipboard commands, select Copy. You can also do this with the keyboard shortcut Ctrl+C.

3 Select the cell or area in which you would like the data to appear.

4 In the Clipboard commands, choose paste: the data will appear in the selected area. You can also do this with the keyboard shortcut Ctrl+V.

If you would like to completely cut the data from one place when it has been moved to another, follow the steps above, but in step 2 select "Cut" and ignore the keyboard shortcuts. The keyboard shortcuts in step 4 will not apply to the cut and paste commands either.

→ Deleting Data

To delete data from a cell or group of cells, or to delete a chart, choose the item or items that you would like to delete and press the delete button on your keyboard. The data or items will disappear. If you decide immediately that you need the data or item back, click the undo button.

30

31

Getting Started with PowerPoint

In this lesson you'll learn about the new features of PowerPoint 2007 as well as how to start, save and close a presentation.

→ What's New in PowerPoint

The new interface that you explored in Word 2007 is back in PowerPoint 2007. The Ribbon navigational structure has replaced the drop-down menus of the past. You'll also find the quick toolbar at the top of the window, near the Office Button, and the view toolbar is in the bottom-right corner of the page.

There are a host of new tools and features available in PowerPoint. For example, when you open the program you're automatically taken to the Home tab where you have a single blank slide available and buttons located in the Ribbon to add more slides.

By studying users' habits, Microsoft has discovered that this is usually the first task that users undertake when they open PowerPoint. The remaining tabs are arranged in the order in which they are most frequently used.

Here are some additional new features and tools:

■ **Quick formatting options:** You have several formatting options in PowerPoint. The Home tab gives you the controls that you need to quickly create and format slides. From the Insert tab you can add a variety of graphics, while from the Design tab you can quickly change the look and feel of your presentation.

■ **Contextual menus for tables and charts:** Contextual menus put everything in context, so if you're working with graphs or charts, appropriate menus appear for those functions. If you're reviewing your document, you're taken to an appropriate menu for that. PowerPoint puts the tools you need in front of you when you need them.

■ **Layout and theme options:** Apply existing layouts and themes or create your own with a few mouse-clicks. Using the Live Preview option, you can view these changes before you commit to them.

- **Animation and effects:** Animation and effects have never been easier to apply to your presentations. Use the Animations tab to quickly add animation and effects to your presentation. If you don't find what you're looking for there, create your own.

- **New presentation options:** The new presentation options in PowerPoint make the program more useful than it's ever been. If you've ever wished you could run a presentation on multiple computers, you're in luck. Now, using the options in the Slide Show Set Up, you can set your presentations to be viewed on multiple monitors or you can change the way the presentation is viewed: as presented by a speaker, as viewed by an individual, or as browsed at a kiosk.

- **Graphics tools:** The graphics tools in PowerPoint are more powerful than ever. When you add a graphic to your presentation, menus that help you design and format your graphic automatically appear. When you've finished formatting your graphics, the tabs disappear so they aren't cluttering your Ribbon. Don't worry, though. Getting them back is as easy as double-clicking on the graphic.

31

- **Publishing options:** Another new feature in PowerPoint is the ability to publish presentations to a slide library, package them for disk and publish to a SharePoint server. These publishing options give you more control than ever for using your presentations in a way that works with your needs.

- **Finalization tools:** Finalization tools help you increase the security of your documents. Add digital signatures, inspect the document, or restrict permissions using the Finalize option on the File menu.

All of the new features of PowerPoint are designed with one purpose: to make it quick and easy for you to create powerful, professional presentations. You can draw from a library of prepared slides or create your own custom slides. And templates make it easy to create a presentation on the fly. It's all part of the plan to make it easier for you to use PowerPoint to achieve professional results.

The new tools and features are also much easier to find because they're no longer buried out of sight. Live Preview lets you see results before you commit to them. Want to insert a chart in your presentation and use data from an existing Excel spreadsheet to populate it? It's easy to do using PowerPoint's graphics tools. And it's all part of the grand (re)design: make it easy to use.

→ Customising PowerPoint

Changing the PowerPoint user interface is about the same as changing the user interface in Word, but you'll find that some of the options are different. Some of the customisation you can do is aesthetic, but some functional customisation is available, too.

As with Word, customisation starts in the File menu, which is located behind the Windows button.

The customisation options in PowerPoint include the following:

- **Personalize:** Use the Personalize menu to change the look and feel of your PowerPoint program. Here you can add or remove tabs from the Ribbon, change the colour scheme of your PowerPoint skin, enable or disable certain functions, and change your user name, initials and language settings.

- **Proofing:** Manage your correcting and formatting options from here. These options include autocorrection settings, spelling correction options for all Office programs and spelling options for PowerPoint.

- **Save:** Manage how (and where) your documents are saved. Saving options include backup information, draft locations and fidelity preservation for document sharing.

- **Advanced:** All of your advanced functions can be found on this screen. Set options for editing, displaying editing elements or document content, accessibility and compatibility using this menu. There are also additional options that occur in other menus as well. These include Print, Save, Preserve Fidelity, Grammar and General Options.

■ **Customization:** Use the Customization menu to change what's included in your Quick Access Toolbar and to create or change keyboard shortcuts. The Quick Access Toolbar is located on the top left of the page, next to the Office Button. This toolbar lets you quickly access some of the most used functions of PowerPoint, such as Save, Undo, Repeat and Quick Print.

■ **Add-Ins:** View and manage your add-ins from this screen.

■ **Trust Center:** This is one of the new features of Office. The Trust Center is where you select the option for the protection of your documents and the security of your PC. You'll find options here for advanced Trust Center settings that include managing publishers, locations, add-ins, ActiveX controls, macro settings, document Action Bar settings and privacy options.

31

Important

It's not recommended that you change any of the options in the Trust Center. These options are pre-set to the most secure settings for your protection. Changing the settings could result in putting your personal information at risk.

■ **Resources:** Additional resources are located on this page of the PowerPoint Options dialogue box. These aren't customisation links but instead are links to Office Online, Office activation, updates, the diagnostics program, contact information for Microsoft, and security and privacy information and policies.

If you don't happen to be one of the people who likes the Windows blue that's the default background colour for all the Office programs, you can change it. To change the colour scheme, follow these steps:

1 Go to **File > PowerPoint Options**.

2 In the PowerPoint Options window that appears, select **Popular**.

3 Click the **Color Scheme** drop-down menu, as shown in Figure 31.1, and select the desired colour.

4 Click **OK** to save your changes and close the **Options** dialogue box.

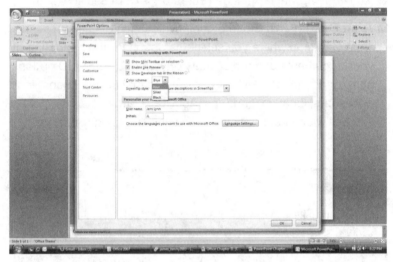

Figure 31.1
Change the background colour of PowerPoint using the PowerPoint Options menu.

→ Starting a New Presentation

The fastest way to create a new presentation in PowerPoint is to open the program. This brings you to a blank slide, from which you can build a presentation. But if you want a little more structure than that, your next option is to use an existing PowerPoint template. As with previous versions of PowerPoint, a few templates come installed with the program. Additional templates can be downloaded from the Microsoft Office website and PowerPoint 2007 makes that even easier than in the past. Presentation options give you the flexibility to create your own presentation from a single blank slide, or to use new templates or templates from previous versions of PowerPoint.

To create a presentation from a template:

1 Click the Office button and select **New**.

2 The **New Presentation** dialogue box appears, as shown in Figure 31.2. Select a presentation option: blank presentation, a PowerPoint 2007 template, or an existing template from a previous version of PowerPoint.

3 Click Create.

Figure 31.2
The New Presentation dialogue box contains all the template options for creating a new presentation.

→ Saving and Closing a Presentation

There is a lot more that you can do with PowerPoint when you're creating your presentations, but you'll learn about that in the following chapters. Right now, you need to know how to save and close a presentation.

By now, you should be familiar with the saving and closing functions of Office. In PowerPoint they work just the same as in Word or Excel.

To save a file:

■ Use the keyboard shortcut **Ctrl+S**.

■ Click the diskette icon in the Quick toolbar.

■ Select the Office button and choose **Save.**

If you have already saved your presentation, these options will just update the file. If you have not previously saved the file, you'll be prompted to create a file name and select a location to which you would like the file saved.

Once you've saved the file, closing it is easy. Click the **X** in the upper right corner or select the **Office** button and choose **Close.**

32

Working with Presentation Views

In this lesson you'll learn how to use Presentation Views, the Outline Pane, the Slide Sorter, the Notes Page and the Slide Show.

→ Understanding Presentation Views

Presentation views are the various ways in which you can view your presentation. You'll find the **Presentation Views** menu on the **Views** tab in PowerPoint. The options available in this menu include:

- **Normal**: Your normal view of a presentation as you're creating or adjusting it. This is the default view.

- **Slide Sorter**: Changes your view to smaller slides with more on a page so you can move them around without scrolling through page after page of slides.

- **Notes Page**: This page is for speaker notes.

- **Slide Show**: This option allows you to run your presentation as a slide show.

- **Slide Master**: Use this view to make changes to the design and layout of your presentation.

- **Handout Master**: Use this view to make changes to the design and layout of your handouts.

- **Notes Master**: Allows you to make changes to the design and layout of speaker notes.

→ Using the Outline Pane

The Outline Pane is an area of PowerPoint where you can design and adjust presentations by their outline. You'll find the Outline Pane tab on the **Slides** task pane to the left of the slide workspace, as shown in Figure 32.1.

The Outline Pane represents the outline of your presentation, based on the slides that you have created and the text on those slides. From the Outline Pane, you can move your slides around and you can change the text on any slide by highlighting the existing text and typing over it.

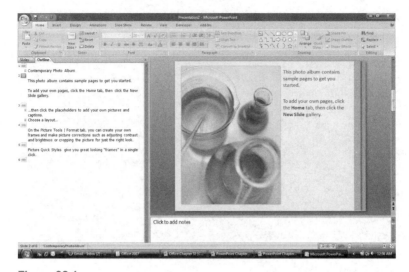

Figure 32.1
The Outline Pane.

The Outline Pane is a simple way for you to edit your presentation slide order and content.

→ Using the Slide Sorter

The Slide Sorter is a feature that you may find you use all the time. The Slide Sorter is shown in Figure 32.2. It allows you to see a smaller view of all your slides in the order they appear in your presentation so that you can change that order if you like.

To change the order of your slides in the Slide Sorter, click and drag slides to the position in the presentation where you would prefer them to appear. When you finish moving the slides around, go back to the Presentation Views section of the View menu and select **Normal** to return to your normal view.

Figure 32.2
Use the Slide Sorter to change the order of your slides.

→ Using the Notes Page

The Notes Page view of your presentation allows you to make changes to the speaker notes for the presentation. Speaker notes are seen by the speaker but not by the audience viewing the presentation. This helps the speaker to ensure he or she is hitting all of the important topics necessary during the presentation.

To work in the Notes Page:

1 Go to **View** and select **Notes Page**, as shown in Figure 32.3.

2 The Notes Page for the slide you are currently working on appears. This page features the slide with a text box for notes below it.

3 Click inside the text box and type whatever notes you would like included.

4 When you've finished making notes, select the **View** tab again and choose **Normal** from the Presentation Views section of the Ribbon.

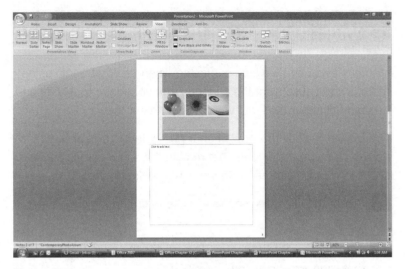

Figure 32.3
The Notes Page contains the speaker's notes for the presentation.

→ Using the Slide Show

The Slide Show feature of PowerPoint allows you to run through a slide show of the presentation you are creating. This capability makes it possible for you to see what your users will see on-screen while you're giving your presentation.

To use the Slide Show feature:

1 Click the **Slide Shown** option on the **Presentation Views** of the View tab.

2 This opens your slide show to the first slide in the series.

3 To advance the slide show, press the right arrow key on your keyboard.

4 When you come to the end of the presentation, press the arrow key again to return to PowerPoint.

→ Understanding and Using Master Views

Master views can be a little confusing when you first begin using them. It's because all of the changes that you make to a slide can be made in either the Final View or the Master View.

The Master View is the view of your presentation that shows design and layout elements that remain the same across all the slides in your presentation. To work in the Master View:

1 Select the slide that you would like to change in the Master View.

2 Click **View > Slide Master**. This opens the Master View for that slide, as shown in Figure 32.4.

3 Make the desired changes to the layout and design of the presentation. When you've finished, click the **View** tab and then select **Normal** to return to the normal view of your document.

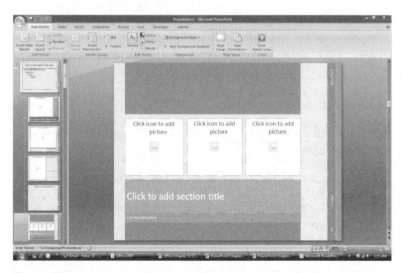

Figure 32.4
Master View.

The Master View works similarly for Handout Master and Notes Master as well. The changes that you make in these views are global changes, meaning they affect the entire presentation.

32

33

Creating a Presentation

In this lesson you'll learn about Slide Libraries,
Colour Schemes and Themes.

→ Using Slide Libraries

One other option that you have for creating a presentation is to use a deck of slides, or a single slide from several decks from a local slide library. A slide library is a group of presentations that has been saved to your SharePoint server for use across the organisation. Any presentation can be saved as part of a slide library.

Slide libraries cut down on the amount of content that you have to recreate. Rather than repeatedly creating the same slides, you can store them in the slide library and then pull one slide or a whole presentation into a new presentation. And you can link the slides in your presentation to their copies on the server so that any changes made are reproduced to the copy of the presentation that you're using.

Slide libraries are managed by SharePoint Server 2007, so if you don't have SharePoint installed, the slide libraries won't be available to you.

→ Using Colour Schemes

Colour adds interest to any presentation. However, you may find that you start with one colour, or there is an existing colour theme for a presentation that you're creating from a template, and you don't like that theme.

You can change colour schemes using these steps:

1. Click anywhere within your presentation.
2. Go to the **Design** tab.
3. From the **Themes** section of the Ribbon, click the **Color** drop-down menu, shown in Figure 33.1.
4. Select the new colour scheme that you would like to use and it is automatically applied to your presentation.

Figure 33.1
Color menu.

If the colour scheme that you would like to use has not already
been created, you can create a new scheme by clicking the
Create New Theme Colors... link in the drop-down menu.

→ Using Themes

Themes are like colour schemes, except they affect the entire
appearance of a presentation, instead of just the colours. You can
change the themes within a presentation to make it look significantly
different without putting too much time into rewriting the information
contained in the presentation. This is helpful if you find that your
presentation design isn't working well for your audience.

To change your presentation theme:

1 Open the presentation you want to change.

2 Select the **Design** tab and you're taken to the design view for
your presentation, as shown in Figure 33.2.

Figure 33.2
Themes are located on the Design tab.

3 From the **Theme** section of the Ribbon, select the new theme that you would like to use. You can scroll through additional themes or select themes from the Internet using the scroll controls on the right side of the Theme box, as shown in Figure 33.3.

Figure 33.3
Additional themes are available online.

4 When you find the theme you want to use, select it and your presentation is changed to reflect that theme.

If you're working with a presentation that started with a blank slide, you can still apply themes using the same steps as above.

→ Working with Text

Whether you're using a template to create your presentation or creating a presentation from a blank slide, there may come a time when you want to change the text on all the slides within the presentation. Maybe you're using a presentation that was created and run through two test groups before you begin using it. Your test groups liked the presentation, but the most common suggestion from both groups was to make the text more readable.

To change your font theme, follow these steps:

1 Place your cursor within the text, anywhere in the presentation.

2 Go to the **Design** tab.

3 Select the **Fonts** drop-down menu, as shown in Figure 33.4.

4 Choose the font that you want to apply to the presentation. When you put your mouse pointer over a font, the Live Preview function shows you how fonts will look in your presentation before you commit to them.

33

If you're creating a presentation using blank styles, you can use either predesigned slides, or you can add text boxes to your slides as needed.

To add a text box:

1 Go to the **Insert** tab and click **Add Text Box**.

2 Then you can draw the text box position and width. The height is automatically defined by what you type into the text box.

Figure 33.4
Use Theme Fonts to change the fonts within an entire presentation.

One more formatting feature that you might find useful is on the Drawing Tools Format menu that appears when you insert a shape that contains text into your presentation. This menu appears automatically. On the Drawing Tools Format menu there are several text formatting options that you've seen before and one that you haven't. This option, shown in Figure 33.5, is the Text Effects menu.

The Text Effects menu gives you options for changing the effects of text within an object or shape. Choose from Shadow, Reflection, Glow, Bevel, 3-D Rotation and Transform.

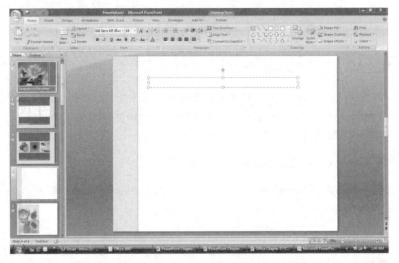

Figure 33.5
The Text Effects menu gives you options for adding interest to your text.

→ Using Formatting Tools

The appearance of the text in your presentation has to perform a specific function: it has to convey information without being distracting. To do this, you may need to use multiple formats within a single presentation. Fortunately, all of the formatting tools that you've used in the past are still available to you.

The main font menu on the Home tab is your all-purpose formatting menu. This menu gives you all of the standard options, such as font type, font size, bold, italics and underline. But what if you need something that's not standard?

In that case, there are two places where additional formatting tools are available. The first is on the Home tab. In addition to the standard formatting options, you'll find a WordArt menu on this tab. The WordArt menu gives you the option to add and edit WordArt in your presentation.

There's also a Paragraph menu on the Home tab. This menu allows you to use formatting options such as bullets and numbers, paragraph styles, fill colours and line spacing to format the text on your slides.

Another option is the Text menu on the Insert tab. On this tab there's a text menu that gives you several additional options for adding and formatting text:

■ **Text box**: Add a text box to any slide.

■ **Header & Footer**: Add headers and/or footers to the slides in a presentation.

■ **WordArt**: Select a WordArt style to apply to selected text.

■ **Date & Time**: Insert the date and/or time into a slide.

■ **Number**: Insert a number into a slide.

■ **Symbol**: Add a symbol to text on a slide.

■ **Object**: Insert an object (such as a PDF document) into your presentation.

34

Working with Graphics

In this lesson you'll learn about adding pictures and clip art, diagrams and charts and bulleted or numbered lists.

→ Adding Pictures and Clip Art

Standard fare for documents and presentations of all types are images and Clip Art. PowerPoint 2007 is no exception.

To insert a picture or Clip Art into your presentation:

1 Go to the **Insert** tab.

2 Select **Picture** or **Clip Art**.

3 Select the image you want to insert and click **Insert**.

4 The image is inserted into the presentation and, as shown in Figure 34.1, the Picture Tools Format menu tab appears.

5 Use these tools to format, change and arrange the picture or Clip Art.

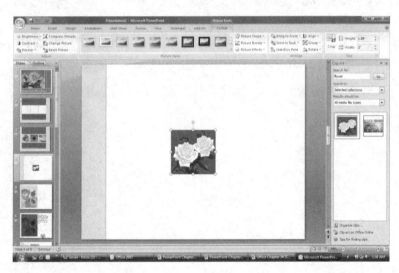

Figure 34.1
Insert a picture or Clip Art and the Picture Tools Format menu tab appears.

You can also use these directions to insert a table or shapes into your presentation. As with other objects, when you add these elements into your presentation, the contextual menus appear so you can change, update, rearrange, or format the elements.

→ Creating Diagrams and Charts

Diagrams show how processes, cycles and relationships work. These elements are useful when you're trying to illustrate how information fits into these processes, but in the past there was no easy way to add a diagram to your presentation.

Adding them to presentations created in PowerPoint 2007 is much easier than before, however. All it takes to add a diagram to your presentation now is for you to select the slide into which you want to insert the diagram, click the Insert tab, then select the diagram that you want to add to the slide from the SmartArt menu.

When the diagram appears, as shown in Figure 34.2, add your own text to complete the visual image.

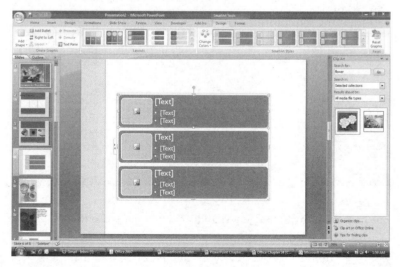

Figure 34.2
Complete the diagram by adding your own text in the boxes provided.

If the diagram you've added has a small picture icon in it, you can also add pictures and Clip Art to the diagram to customise it. Further customisation of colours and effects can be added from the Design tab. Use themes to consistently change colours, add backgrounds and create visual appeal in your diagrams.

Creating charts works in much the same way that creating diagrams works. The difference is that charts generally draw from numerical information rather than text information. To insert a chart into your presentation:

1 Select the slide on which you would like the chart to appear.

2 Go to the **Insert** tab and select **Chart**.

3 The **Insert Chart** dialogue box appears, as shown in Figure 34.3.

4 Then click OK.

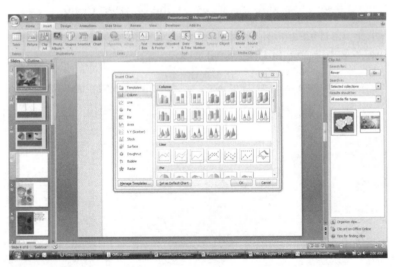

Figure 34.3
Select the chart type that you want to insert in the presentation.

5 The chart is inserted into your presentation and a sample Microsoft Excel worksheet containing information that populates the chart appears.

6 Enter the information that you want to include in the chart and then save and close the Excel workbook.

7 Now your chart is complete and you can reformat it in whatever manner works best with your presentation.

Once you've created the chart, the Chart Tools tabs appear. They are Design, Layout and Format. Use these tabs to change and customise the chart that you've just created. You can also use them to change, update, or add to the data source for the chart.

→ Inserting Bulleted or Numbered Lists

One of the more interesting new features in PowerPoint is what you can do with bulleted and numbered lists. Adding a plain bulleted or numbered list is easy enough: click the bulleted or numbered list button on the Paragraph menu. But PowerPoint now offers SmartArt that you can use in place of bulleted lists – you might never use plain bulleted lists again.

Creating a bulleted or numbered list is easy:

1 Place your cursor at the location on the slide where you want the list to appear.

2 Click the bulleted or numbered list icon from the Home tab.

3 Your slide is automatically formatted for a bulleted or numbered list.

34

→ Converting Lists to Diagrams

You've learned about diagrams and charts, but you still haven't seen one of the coolest features of PowerPoint 2007: using a list to create a diagram in just two clicks. Honest, it's really that simple. Here's how:

1 Create a slide in your presentation. You can use just about any layout that includes text capabilities to create the slide.

2 Right-click anywhere within the list area.

3 From the list that appears, highlight **Convert to SmartArt**, and as shown in Figure 34.4, the SmartArt options appear.

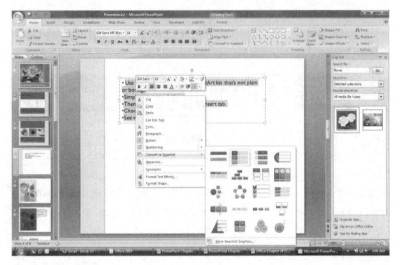

Figure 34.4
Like magic, the SmartArt options appear when you highlight Convert to SmartArt.

4 Click the thumbnail that represents the SmartArt diagram that suits your presentation: it will automatically be inserted on your slide in place of the list that you originally created, as shown in Figure 34.5. The text list is also opened automatically so you can change any of the points included in the original list.

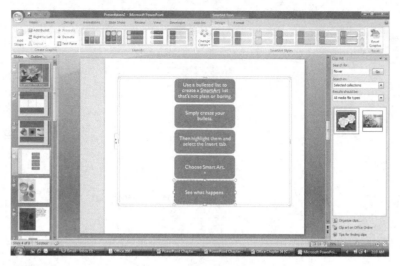

Figure 34.5
The SmartArt diagram replaces the list you created.

Important

One limitation of the SmartArt feature that you should be aware of is the tendency of PowerPoint to automatically convert all of the text outside the title area of your slide into SmartArt diagrams. Even if you highlight only the lines that you want converted to SmartArt, the program will still convert all of the text, highlighted and unhighlighted, and merge it into the SmartArt diagram.

34

Once you have inserted the SmartArt diagram into your slide, you are automatically taken to the Design tab where you can change the diagram layout and style or change the colours of the diagram with a few mouse-clicks. Live Preview is also available from this tab, making it possible for you to preview your results before you commit to them.

35

Adding Media to Your Presentation

In this lesson you'll learn about working with sounds, animations and transitions.

→ Working with Sounds

Sound, when used sparingly, adds a nice element to your presentation. For example, if you want to get the audience's attention at the beginning of a presentation, you can add an upbeat audio track to the title slide. The audio track will alert attendees that the presentation is about to begin.

You can also record your own audio to add to a presentation. However, recording your own audio track requires you to have a microphone attached to your computer.

If you want to add audio to your presentation, follow these steps:

1 Select the slide to which you'd like to add the audio file.

2 Go to the **Insert** tab and select the **Sound** command.

3 As Figure 35.1 shows, you'll be given four options for adding audio to your presentation.

4 Select the desired audio option.

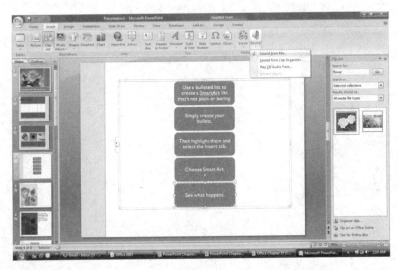

Figure 35.1
Select the type of audio file that you would like to attach to the slide.

Once you select an audio option, the menu or dialogue box appears for that option. Each option is slightly different. For example, if you select **Sound from File**, you're taken to a dialogue box that allows you to select the sound (stored on your hard drive) that you want to include. But if you choose to insert a recording, the Recording dialogue box appears.

After you select the sound that you want to include in your presentation, you may also be prompted to set the attributes of the sound. One of the options that you may be prompted to choose is whether the sound should start on a click or automatically.

You'll also be taken to the Sound Tools Options tab. From this tab you can set additional attributes for the sound you've inserted, including whether the sound should loop or play just one time and at what volume the sound should be.

Important

When you insert a sound into your presentation, a small icon that looks like a speaker may appear on the slide. This icon indicates that there is a sound clip attached to the slide. To hide that icon, right-click it and select **Send to back**. The icon will then be placed behind other elements on the screen. This is most effective when the icon is sent behind a picture or textbox that will completely hide the icon.

35

→ Adding Animation

Another element that makes PowerPoint presentation interesting is animation. Without animation, a presentation is nothing more than a boring set of slides. However, when you add animation, you have slides that come together in pieces, that perform some automated function automatically, or that appear on a click, as you're discussing the elements of the slide.

Here are the steps to add or change the animation on a slide:

1 Navigate to the slide to which you want to add animation.

2 Click the Animations tab, shown in Figure 35.2.

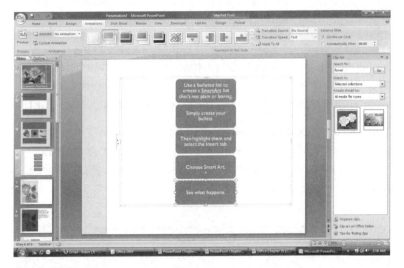

Figure 35.2
Animation effects are controlled from the Animations tab.

3 Select the animation that you want to add to the slide.

You can also add animation to elements within a slide rather than to the whole slide by clicking on the element that you want to animate and then selecting an animation effect for the element.

Timesaver tip

Animation for each slide, whether it's the whole slide that's animated or an element on the slide, is indicated by a small star shown next to the slide in the slide preview. If you click the star, the animation is previewed in Design view.

In some cases, the animation that you want to include in your presentation isn't predesigned. If that's the case, you can create custom animation by selecting the object or slide that you want to animate and then choosing the Custom Animation option. The dialogue box shown in Figure 35.3 is displayed.

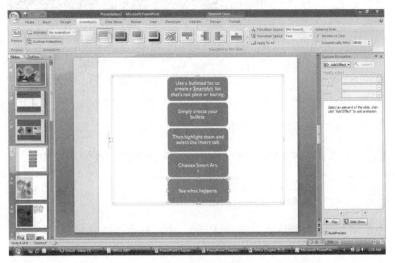

Figure 35.3
The Custom Animation dialogue box allows you to set the elements of animation that you want to include in a slide or object.

Using the Custom Animation options you can add animation or remove it, set it to start on a click or automatically, and set the speed of the animation or reorder it (for multiple elements of animation).

One last animation feature that you may want to be aware of is the Transition Animation. Transition Animation is the animation that occurs when you move from one slide to another. You can have slides fly in, fade in, or one of several other options. The Transition Animation menu is located on the Animations tab.

When you add custom animation, the animation is indicated in the Design view by numbers on each slide or element where the animation takes place. The numbers indicate the order in which

35

the animation will occur. You can also select transition for individual elements to occur simultaneously by selecting With Previous from the Start menu.

→ Using Transitions

One last element of animation: the transition. The transition is the change from one slide to the next. If you've ever seen a PowerPoint presentation where each slide seemed to fade in or fly in, then you've seen a transition.

To add a transition to a slide:

1 Open the presentation to which you would like to add the transition.

2 Select the **Animations** tab.

3 In the **Transition** section of the Animations tab, select the transition type you would like to use.

4 Then add a sound (if desired) and transition speed.

5 When you've finished, select **Apply to all** to apply that transition to all of the slides in your presentation.

You can preview how your transitions and other animations will look by viewing a slide show of your presentation.

36

Finishing Your Presentation

In this lesson you'll learn about the Quick Print Option and packaging your presentation for CD.

→ Using the Quick Print Option

Once you've completed your presentation, it's time to start
thinking about how you're going to distribute it. Often, people will
show the presentation live at a conference, meeting, or trade
show, but then they will also hand out notes about the
presentation or even print copies of it.

To use Quick Print to print a copy of your presentation, follow
these steps:

1 Click the Office button and select **Print > Quick Print**, as
shown in Figure 36.1.

2 If you have not saved your file before now, you will be
prompted to save. Once the presentation has been saved,
the file will be transferred to the printer.

Quick Print is a clever feature that lets you quickly print your
whole presentation. However, there may be times when you want
to print something other than just the presentation.

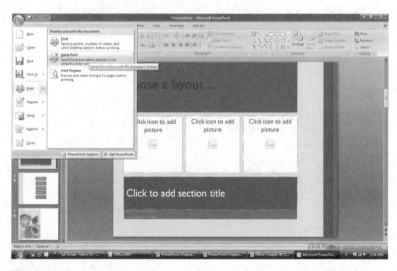

Figure 36.1
Use Quick Print to print a copy of the presentation.

→ Choosing What to Print

Knowing what to print when you're printing your presentation is sometimes a chore. You have to ask yourself, what is the purpose for the paper copies of the presentation? Once you figure that out, you can choose to print only the presentation, print the notes or handouts, or print any combination of the three.

To print all or part of your presentation follow these steps:

1 From your open presentation, click the Office button and select **Print**.

2 Select **Print** again from the menu that appears. This opens the **Print** dialogue box.

3 In the dialogue box, use the drop down menus to choose the printer you would like to send your presentation to, how many copies of the presentation to print, what elements (i.e. slides, handouts, notes pages, or outline view) to print.

4 When you've finished making your selections, click **Preview** to preview what your presentation will look like when printed.

5 When you've finished previewing your file, click the **Print** icon, confirm your selections, and then click **OK** to send the presentation to the printer.

→ Packaging Your Presentation for CD

36

One additional feature of PowerPoint 2007 that you might find useful is the ability to package your presentation to be burned to CD. Storing your presentation on CD makes it easy to share and archive. But in the past, burning a presentation to CD was less than user friendly. Today, even with charting and graphics that include imbedded information from other sources, you can save a CD-ready file, or burn your presentation to CD at the click of a button. Here's how:

1 Once you've completed your presentation, select File and click **Publish > Package for CD**.

2 The **Package for CD** dialogue box appears, as shown in Figure 36.2.

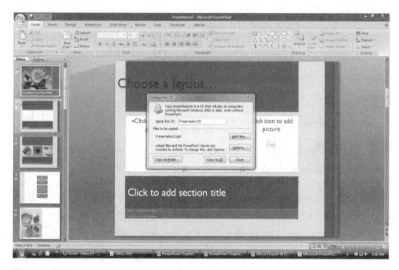

Figure 36.2
The Package for CD dialogue box.

3 Select the desired options: name your CD, select any additional files that you want to save, then click the Options button. (Don't worry about embedded files, the program handles that.)

4 In the Options menu, you can choose the presentation type, select the "Include these files" options and set security and privacy.

5 When you've made your selections, click to either save the finished file or burn it to CD and you're done.

37

What's New with Access 2007

In this lesson you'll learn about the new features of Access 2007 including the Ribbon, the Quick Access Toolbar and Navigation Pane.

→ Using the Ribbon

With Microsoft Access 2007, you can manage, track and share information by using data from different sources. Access 2007 is more intuitive than previous versions because it uses the Ribbon. This easy-to-follow, tabbed concept from Microsoft makes finding and using commands simple, no matter what level of experience you have with Access.

The Ribbon is a vertical bar across the top of the window that replaces menus and toolbars previously used in Access. Within this bar are tabs that hold various commands you will use. Depending on the task or object you are working on, a contextual command tab groups together commands that are related to your current activity.

Jargon buster

Access objects are the items that make up the database. These include tables, forms, queries and reports.

Figure 37.1 shows the command tabs located in the Ribbon of a newly opened Access database.

Each command tab logically groups together commands to simplify your work. In Figure 37.1, the Home tab displays seven groups: Views, Clipboard, Font, Rich Text, Records, Sort & Filter, and Find. You can change almost every item directly from the Microsoft Office Buttons or their drop-down lists. To remove gridlines, for example, you would click on the Gridlines Button and select "None" from the drop-down list.

For commands not immediately visible in the Microsoft Office Button or its drop-down list, click on the small, angled arrow in the bottom right corner of the Microsoft Office Button.

Figure 37.1:
The Ribbon helps you easily locate the command you need.

A dialogue box with additional commands, shown in Figure 37.2, appears when you click the angled arrow in the bottom right corner of the Microsoft Office Button. You will want to review the Microsoft Office Buttons for a better understanding of where commands are launched from.

Figure 37.2
Additional commands.

The Ribbon displays only the commands associated with the task you are currently working on. Command tabs change as your activity changes, so you can find the Microsoft Office Buttons you need quickly and easily.

→ Take Advantage of the Quick Access Toolbar

The Quick Access Toolbar, shown in Figure 37.3, makes your time using Access even more efficient and specific to your needs. This small toolbar, which is located immediately above the Ribbon, can be customised for the commands you use often.

You can use the Quick Access Toolbar drop-down menu to add commands that make you more productive when using Access. To add a command to the toolbar:

37

Figure 37.3
The Quick Access Toolbar can be customised for the way you work.

1 Click the down arrow next to **Customize Quick Access Toolbar**, as shown in Figure 37.4.

2 Click the command to add it to your toolbar.

Figure 37.4
A drop-down menu helps you customise your Quick Access Toolbar quickly.

To add a Ribbon command to the Quick Access Toolbar, follow these steps:

1 Right-click on the command you want to add.

2 Select **Add to Quick Access Toolbar**.

Timesaver tip

To move the Quick Access Toolbar below the Ribbon, click the Customize Quick Access Toolbar down arrow, then select Show Below the Ribbon.

One other way to add commands to your Quick Access Toolbar is by using the Access Options. The steps are:

1 Click the **Microsoft Office Button**.

2 Click **Access Options** to see the dialogue box shown in Figure 37.5.

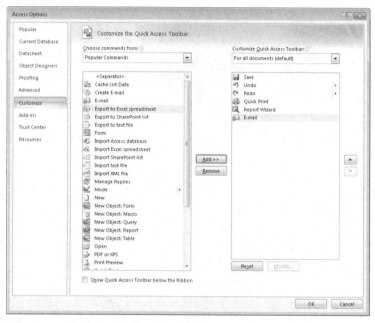

Figure 37.5
Use the Access Options to customise the Quick Access Toolbar.

3 Select **Customize**.

4 In **Choose commands from**, select the appropriate category.

5 Below **Choose commands from**, select the command you want to add. Click **Add** to move the command to the column on the right. Continue adding commands as needed. To remove a command, click on the item in the right-hand column and select **Remove**.

6 Click **OK**.

37

→ Working with the Navigation pane

Located below the Ribbon is the Navigation pane. This new
Access 2007 feature remains on the left side of the window until
you collapse it. All objects that correspond with new or existing
databases appear in the Navigation pane and are categorised and
grouped, as shown in Figure 37.6.

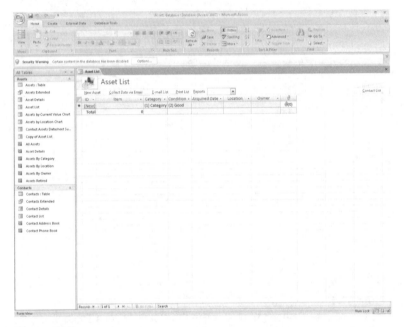

Figure 37.6
The Navigation pane shows all database objects by category and
group.

Tables and Related Views is the default category, while All Tables
is the default group for this category. If an object is based on
more than one table, it will appear in the groups for each table.
Selecting another category using the drop-down menu will group
your objects differently; you can use the down arrow at the top of
the Navigation pane, as shown in Figure 37.7. You can also use
up and down arrows to collapse or expand a group.

Figure 37.7
Categories can be selected by using a drop-down menu in the Navigation pane.

Timesaver tip

You can manage objects in a database directly from the Navigation pane. This pane has replaced the switchboard previously used in Access. While some switchboards created in earlier versions of Access may work in Access 2007, limitations often occur.

The Navigation pane consists of five key areas that appear as you work and includes database objects and their shortcuts.

The first three areas are the menu, groups and database objects. The Shutter Bar Open/Close Button, located next to the menu, opens and collapses the Navigation pane. Open space is the final key area in Access 2007. A right-click in the Navigation pane open space opens a menu with tasks you can use for the objects in each group.

37

→ Understanding the New File Format

When you save files in Access 2007, the new default file format is .accdb. Previous versions of Access used the file extension .mdb.

The new file format includes improved encryption methods, attachment data types, multi-valued fields and memo field history tracking. The format also offers stronger integration with Windows SharePoint Services and Microsoft Office Outlook 2007.

Jargon buster

Encryption turns text into non-readable information so that sensitive data remains secure.

To maximise space, the attachment data types feature automatically compresses attachments stored in your database. Multi-valued fields let you select and store more than one choice for a field without an advanced database design. These integrate well with Microsoft Windows SharePoint Services 3.0. Memo field history tracking allows you to retain a history of changes to a memo field in a database so you can see what happened and when.

Converting files from earlier versions of Access to the new format will provide all the newest features and functions. For example, you cannot make design changes to a file in Access 95 or Access 97 format when you open it in Access 2007. However, you can still save the database as an .mdb file, if needed.

Timesaver tip

Access 2007 allows you to open Access files with the .mdb extension though you may not be able to use the newer features. Earlier versions of Access cannot open files saved in the new .accdb format.

→ Convert a Database to an Access 2007 File

Here are the steps to convert a database created in an earlier version of Access into an Access 2007 file. After you have opened Access 2007:

1 Click the Microsoft Office Button.

2 Click **Open**.

3 When the Open dialogue box appears, select and open the database that you want to convert.

4 Select the Microsoft Office Button, then point to **Save As**.

5 Under **Save the database in another format**, click Access 2007 Database.

6 In the File name box of the Save As dialogue box, enter a file name or use the file name supplied.

7 Click **Save**.

37

38

Access 2007 Fundamentals

In this lesson you'll learn about opening, saving and exiting Access.

In this lesson, you will learn how to open and exit Access and how to exit a database and you will get acquainted with the displays, function keys and views.

→ Opening Access

You can open Access 2007 in a number of ways. To create a new database from scratch, use the Start button in Windows Vista. Follow these steps:

1 Go to Start.

2 Select **All Programs**.

3 Select **Microsoft Office**.

4 Select **Microsoft Office Access 2007**.

Windows Vista places programs that you open in the Start menu, unless you open several programs. Here are the steps to "pin" Access 2007 in the Start menu so you can find it easily. After you have Access 2007 open:

1 Go to Start.

2 Right-click Microsoft Access 2007.

3 Click **Pin to Start Menu**, as shown in Figure 38.1, to place Access 2007 in the upper part of the Start menu.

You will see the "Getting Started with Microsoft Access" screen shown in Figure 38.2 when you open Access 2007.

Figure 38.1
You can add programs to your Start menu.

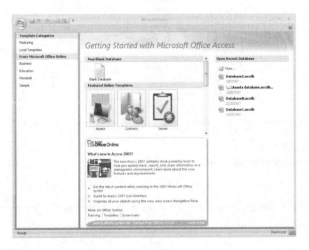

Figure 38.2
The "Getting Started" screen.

→ Working with the Northwind Sample Database

The Northwind 2007 database is a sample database to let you see many features in Access 2007. For this screen to appear:

1 Click **Local Templates** under Template Categories.

2 Click **Northwind 2007** under Local Templates towards the centre of your screen, as shown in Figure 38.3.

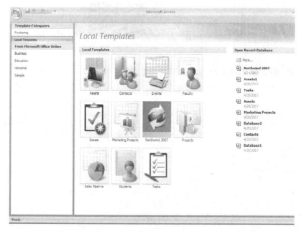

Figure 38.3
Select the sample Northwind database.

3 Select **Create** on the right side of your screen. It may take a few moments for the database template to appear.

4 From the Northwind database screen, a startup screen will appear. If you see a security warning, you need to enable all content in the database. To do this:

5 Click **Options**.

6 Select "Enable this content", as shown in Figure 38.4.

Figure 38.4
Enable the content to proceed.

7 Click **OK**.

8 When the Login Dialogue box appears, click Login on any employee you choose.

Timesaver tip

With Access 2007, you can create a database from a template. You will find several template options in the Getting Started with Microsoft Office Access screen.

→ Function Keys

Access 2007 offers you several keyboard shortcut keys. Use the Help and Support information for keyboard shortcuts to learn how to work more efficiently in Access 2007. You may also refer to the shortcuts in this chart, noting that some shortcuts work only in certain Access views or areas. If one of these shortcuts does not work, you need to change the view or area you are in; Help and Support can provide more details.

38

Press	To perform this function
Ctrl+N	Open a new database
Ctrl+O	Open an existing database
ALT+F4	Exit Access 2007
Ctrl+P	Print the current or selected object
F12	Open the Save As dialogue box
F11	Open or close the Navigation pane
F1	Open Access 2007 Help and Support
F4	Switch to the property sheet
F5	Switch to Form view from the Design view
F6	Switch between upper and lower portions of a window *or* cycle through the areas in the Design view of a table

→ View Options

This is a brief overview of the four primary views in Access 2007: Form, Layout, Datasheet and Design.

■ **Form**: This view shows the actual form as readers will see it.

■ **Layout**: With this view, you can arrange data on the page and make design changes to forms. Generally, this is the view you will use to perform tasks that affect the appearance of a form.

■ **Datasheet**: You can enter data in this view by typing, pasting, or importing information; data must be entered in adjacent rows and columns.

■ **Design**: Use this detailed view to create the structure and set the field properties for a new table.

To change your view while in a database:

1 From the Home tab, click **View** in the Views group.

2 Click the view you want to see.

→ Saving in Access

Follow these steps to save a database created in Access 2007:

1 Select the Microsoft Office Button.

2 Select **Save As** and select **Access 2007 Database**, as shown in Figure 38.5.

Figure 38.5
Select Access 2007 Database.

3 Click **Yes** on the warning telling you that all open objects must be closed prior to converting to a different version.

4 In the Save As window, type in the name of your database in **File Name**.

5 You should Save as a Microsoft Office Access 2007 Database (*.accdb).

6 Click **Save**.

38

→ Exiting Access

After you have saved your database, you can exit Access 2007 through the Microsoft Office Button. Follow these steps to exit:

1 Select the Microsoft Office Button.

2 Click **Exit Access**.

Timesaver tip

You can exit Access 2007 quickly by clicking the X in the top right corner of the Access window.

39

Understanding Access 2007

In this lesson you'll learn about databases and objects, tables, forms, queries, reports, macros, modules and the Sandbox Operating Mode.

→ Databases and Objects

Databases are created from pieces of information collected in a certain structure and stored as records on a computer. A database object in Access 2007 can be a form, table, column, view, report, macro, or module. These objects, which recognise where and how the information is stored, can be saved in more than one way. For example, a table may also be saved as a form.

Tables

In Access 2007, tables are used to organise information in lists of rows and columns. One table may be used for a simple database, but numerous tables may be used to store information for an extremely complex database.

While tables and spreadsheets may look similar, they store and organise information differently. Tables store pieces of information individually, while spreadsheets store information on a single spreadsheet.

A record is made up of a row; within that record can be a number of columns that are called fields. For instance, Figure 39.1 shows that Company A (record) includes various fields (columns) such as name, job title, business phone number, fax number, etc.

Forms

You can use forms to see, enter and edit data easily in Access tables. If you are tracking "Students", for instance, you can have a form that keeps all the student data. You can then program and add a command button to the form to get each student's attendance records quickly.

Forms are also helpful if you need to share your database with others and want to ensure data accuracy and integrity. You simply create forms that display only the fields that others need and limit the number of actions they can perform.

ID	Company	Last Name	First Name	Job Title	Business Ph	Fax Number	Address	City	State/Provin	ZIP/Postal C	Country/Reg	Wel
1	Company A	Bedecs	Anna	Owner	(123)555-0100	(123)555-0101	123 1st Street	Seattle	WA	99999	USA	
2	Company B	Gratacos Solsol	Antonio	Owner	(123)555-0100	(123)555-0101	123 2nd Street	Boston	MA	99999	USA	
3	Company C	Axen	Thomas	Purchasing Representat	(123)555-0100	(123)555-0101	123 3rd Street	Los Angelas	CA	99999	USA	
4	Company D	Lee	Christina	Purchasing Manager	(123)555-0100	(123)555-0101	123 4th Street	New York	NY	99999	USA	
5	Company E	O'Donnell	Martin	Owner	(123)555-0100	(123)555-0101	123 5th Street	Minneapolis	MN	99999	USA	
6	Company F	Pérez-Olaeta	Francisco	Purchasing Manager	(123)555-0100	(123)555-0101	123 6th Street	Milwaukee	WI	99999	USA	
7	Company G	Xie	Ming-Yang	Owner	(123)555-0100	(123)555-0101	123 7th Street	Boise	ID	99999	USA	
8	Company H	Andersen	Elizabeth	Purchasing Representat	(123)555-0100	(123)555-0101	123 8th Street	Portland	OR	99999	USA	
9	Company I	Mortensen	Sven	Purchasing Manager	(123)555-0100	(123)555-0101	123 9th Street	Salt Lake City	UT	99999	USA	
10	Company J	Wacker	Roland	Purchasing Manager	(123)555-0100	(123)555-0101	123 10th Street	Chicago	IL	99999	USA	
11	Company K	Krschne	Peter	Purchasing Manager	(123)555-0100	(123)555-0101	123 11th Street	Miami	FL	99999	USA	
12	Company L	Edwards	John	Purchasing Manager	(123)555-0100	(123)555-0101	123 12th Street	Las Vegas	NV	99999	USA	
13	Company M	Ludick	Andre	Purchasing Representat	(123)555-0100	(123)555-0101	456 13th Street	Memphis	TN	99999	USA	
14	Company N	Grilo	Carlos	Purchasing Representat	(123)555-0100	(123)555-0101	456 14th Street	Denver	CO	99999	USA	
15	Company O	Kupkova	Helena	Purchasing Manager	(123)555-0100	(123)555-0101	456 15th Street	Honolulu	HI	99999	USA	
16	Company P	Goldschmidt	Daniel	Purchasing Representat	(123)555-0100	(123)555-0101	456 16th Street	San Francisco	CA	99999	USA	
17	Company Q	Bagel	Jean Philippe	Owner	(123)555-0100	(123)555-0101	456 17th Street	Seattle	WA	99999	USA	
18	Company R	Autier Miconi	Catherine	Purchasing Representat	(123)555-0100	(123)555-0101	456 18th Street	Boston	MA	99999	USA	
19	Company S	Eggerer	Alexander	Accounting Assistant	(123)555-0100	(123)555-0101	789 19th Street	Los Angelas	CA	99999	USA	
20	Company T	Li	George	Purchasing Manager	(123)555-0100	(123)555-0101	789 20th Street	New York	NY	99999	USA	
21	Company U	Tham	Bernard	Accounting Manager	(123)555-0100	(123)555-0101	789 21th Street	Minneapolis	MN	99999	USA	
22	Company V	Ramos	Luciana	Purchasing Assistant	(123)555-0100	(123)555-0101	789 22th Street	Milwaukee	WI	99999	USA	
23	Company W	Entin	Michael	Purchasing Manager	(123)555-0100	(123)555-0101	789 23th Street	Portland	OR	99999	USA	
24	Company X	Hasselberg	Jonas	Owner	(123)555-0100	(123)555-0101	789 24th Street	Salt Lake City	UT	99999	USA	
25	Company Y	Rodman	John	Purchasing Manager	(123)555-0100	(123)555-0101	789 25th Street	Chicago	IL	99999	USA	
26	Company Z	Liu	Run	Accounting Assistant	(123)555-0100	(123)555-0101	789 26th Street	Miami	FL	99999	USA	
27	Company AA	Toh	Karen	Purchasing Manager	(123)555-0100	(123)555-0101	789 27th Street	Las Vegas	NV	99999	USA	
28	Company BB	Raghav	Amritansh	Purchasing Manager	(123)555-0100	(123)555-0101	789 28th Street	Memphis	TN	99999	USA	
29	Company CC	Lee	Soo Jung	Purchasing Manager	(123)555-0100	(123)555-0101	789 29th Street	Denver	CO	99999	USA	
(New)												

Figure 39.1
Records and fields are made up of rows and columns in
Access 2007 tables.

Queries

The query feature helps you gather information from your
database. This helpful feature allows you to find information from
several different tables and places it in a single datasheet so you
can view all the information in one place. It also lets you filter the
data from a query so you will see only the information you need.

You can use the query feature in two ways: a select query simply
pulls data you ask for; an action query pulls the requested data
and performs a task you request.

Timesaver tip

The Query Wizard offers four types of queries, depending on the
information you need.

Reports

In Access 2007, you can use reports to gather information from
your tables in a format that is easy to read. If you want to check
your product inventory, for example, you can run a report with
that specific information, as seen in Figure 39.2.

39

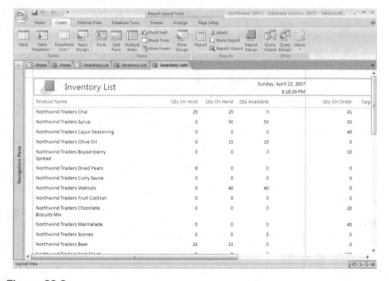

Figure 39.2
Sample report.

You can run reports that can be viewed on the screen, exported to other programs, sent as e-mails, or printed.

Macros

Macros save you time by executing actions for tasks you perform regularly. For example, if you run a certain query every week, you can create a macro to set up and run the query when you click a button. Macros can automate nearly every action you want to perform. Access 2007 provides a list of common actions for you to choose from.

Modules

While modules are similar to macros, they require you to use a programming language, Visual Basic for Applications (VBA), to write the program. Modules are not used often because of the intricacy involved in setting them up.

→ The Sandbox Operating Mode

The Access 2007 default sandbox mode protects your computer by blocking expressions that are considered to be unsafe. An unsafe expression includes properties or functions that malicious users could use to gain entry into your computer's files, drives, or other resources.

Expressions such as "Kill" or "Shell" are considered unsafe because they can damage data and files on a computer. Because the sandbox mode is the default, these expressions will always be blocked unless you disable the mode. You can change a registry key for certain unsafe expressions to run, if you trust the source.

39

→ Change the Registry Key

Important

Enable the content in the database that you are changing the registry key for before beginning this process.

1 Close all the Access databases that you want to disable the sandbox mode on.

In Windows Vista:

2 Select the Start button and point to **All Programs**.

3 Click **Accessories**.

4 Click **Run**. In the Run dialogue box, type regedit.

5 Click **OK**.

6 In the Registry Editor window that opens, expand the HKEY_LOCAL_MACHINE folder in the left pane and navigate to the following registry key: **\Software\Microsoft\Office\ 12.0\Access Connectivity Engine\Engines**

7 In the right pane, double-click **SandboxMode** under **Name**.

8 When the Edit DWORD Value dialogue box appears, change the value from 3 to 2 in the Value Data field.

9 Click **OK**.

10 Close the Registry Editor.

Timesaver tip

Values for the registry range from 0 (most permissive) to 3 (least permissive). To disable the sandbox at all times, use 0; to keep the sandbox mode for Access 2007 but no other programs, use 1; to set the sandbox mode for non-Access programs but *not* Access, use 2; to set the sandbox mode for use at all times and with all programs, use 3.

39

40

Working with Security Settings

In this lesson you'll learn about trusted locations and encrypting databases.

→ Trust Center

From the Trust Center, you can adjust security settings, change trusted locations, establish your security options and perform other security-related tasks. The Trust Center also protects your databases by disabling content it considers to be dangerous to your computer.

If Access views any code or components unsafe, it will disable them and display a message bar to let you know the action taken. You determine the next action by telling Access to trust the database for the remainder of your current session, trust the database permanently, as shown in Figure 40.1, or disable the database.

Figure 40.1
Trust the database.

To trust the database for the current session when you see the message bar:

1 Select **Options**.

2 Select **Enable this content**, as shown in Figure 40.2.

3 Select **OK**.

You can follow these steps to trust the database permanently:

1 Click **Options** on the message bar.

2 Click **Open the Trust Center** in the Security Alert.

3 Click **Trusted Locations** in the Trust Center, as shown in Figure 40.3.

4 Click **Add new location**.

5 Type the file path and folder name in the Microsoft Office Trust Location dialogue box. This will be the trusted location of the database.

Figure 40.2
When Access disables content it considers to be unsafe, you will see a
security alert with options to trust or to disable the database content.

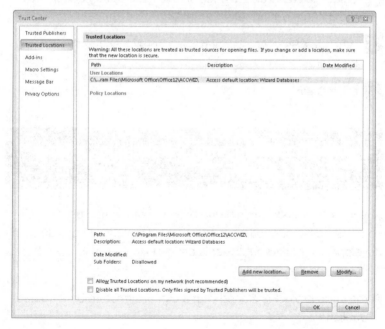

Figure 40.3
Trust Center.

40

6 Click **OK**.

7 Click OK in the Trust Center.

These steps will allow you to finish the process of permanently trusting the database:

1 While in the database, select the Microsoft Office Button.

2 Select **Save As** and choose an available option under "Save the database in another format".

3 When the Save As dialogue box appears, select the trusted location.

4 Click **Save**.

→ Adding or Removing a Developer from a Trusted Location

Anyone who works within a database to create macros, ActiveX controls, add-ins, or other application extensions is considered a developer. A trusted publisher is defined as a reputable developer who ensures that:

■ the code project is signed with a digital signature by a trusted publisher

■ the digital signature is valid as well as current

■ the certificate for the digital signature is issued by a reputable certificate authority.

Follow these steps to add a developer to a trusted location:

1 Open the Security Alert.

2 Select "Trust all documents from this publisher".

3 Select OK.

> **Important**
>
> The only time you are offered the option to "Trust all documents from this publisher" is when Access determines the digital signature is valid. Access will warn you if no signature is present or if it is not valid. Never enable the content or trust the publisher unless you are confident of the source of the database.

Follow these steps to remove a developer from a trusted location:

1 Select the Microsoft Office Button.

2 Select **Access Options**.

3 Select **Trust Center**.

4 Select **Trust Center Settings**.

5 Select **Trusted Publishers**.

6 Select the name to be removed in the Prior Trusted Sources list.

7 Select **Remove**.

→ Changing a Trusted Location

Follow these steps to change a trusted location:

1 Select the Microsoft Office Button.

2 Select **Access Options**.

3 Select **Trust Center**.

40

4 Select **Trust Center Settings**.

5 Select **Trusted Locations**.

6 Select the trusted location under Path that you need to change, as shown in Figure 40.4.

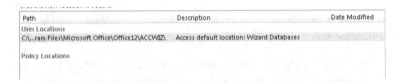

Figure 40.4
Select the trusted location.

7 Select **Modify**.

8 Select **OK**.

9 In the Path box, choose the folder that will be your new trusted location, as shown in Figure 40.5.

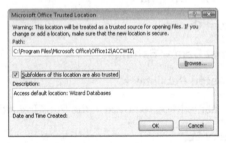

Figure 40.5
Select new trusted location.

10 Select "Subfolders of this location are also trusted" if you want to add subfolders.

11 Define the purpose of the trusted location in the Description box.

12 Click **OK**.

→ Encrypting Your Database

In Access 2007, encrypted data is unreadable unless a password is used. Follow these steps to encrypt a database with a password:

1 Select the Microsoft Office Button.

2 Select **Open**.

3 Find and choose the file you want to open.

4 Select the down arrow on the Open button, as shown in Figure 40.6.

Figure 40.6
Open menu.

40

5 Select **Open Exclusive**.

6 In the Database Tools tab, choose **Encrypt with Password** in the Database Tools group, as shown in Figure 40.7.

Figure 40.7
Encrypt with Password.

7 Type the password in the Set Database Password dialogue box. Enter the information a second time in the Verify box. Click OK.

Important

Access 2007 offers encryption for .accdb files only. This new feature is a stronger encryption code that hides information and protects you from unauthorised use of your database.

→ Open an Encrypted Database

Follow these steps to decrypt your database:

1 Open the encrypted database.

2 Type in your password at the prompt.

Important

You cannot retrieve a password for an encrypted database. Be sure to write down your password and keep it in a safe place so you can find it easily.

→ Remove a Password from an Encrypted Database

If you need to remove a password from a database:

1 Click the Microsoft Office Button.

2 Click **Open**.

3 Find and select the file you want to open.

4 Click the down arrow on the Open button.

5 Click **Open Exclusive**.

6 From the Database Tools tab, choose **Decrypt Database** in the Database Tools group, as shown in Figure 40.8.

Figure 40.8
Decrypt Database.

7 Type your password in the Unset Database Password dialogue box.

8 Click **OK**.

→ Using the Package-and-Sign Feature

To make it easier for others to trust your database, you can use the package-and-sign feature in Access 2007. For databases that have the file extensions .accdb or .accde, Access allows you to package and add a digital signature to the file, then distribute the signed package. At least one security certificate must exist.

40

Follow these steps to create a self-signed security certificate:

1 Click **Start** in Microsoft Windows Vista.

2 Click **All Programs**.

3 Click **Microsoft Office**.

4 Click **Microsoft Office Tools**.

5 Click Digital Certificate for VBA Projects as shown in Figure 40.9.

```
    Ipswitch WS_FTP Pro
    Linksys Wireless-G PCI Network Adapter
    Logitech
    Lotus Applications
    Lotus SmartSuite
    Maintenance
    Microsoft Mouse
    Microsoft Office
        Microsoft Office Access 2007
        Microsoft Office Excel 2007
        Microsoft Office FrontPage 2003
        Microsoft Office Outlook 2007
        Microsoft Office PowerPoint 2007
        Microsoft Office Project 2003
        Microsoft Office Publisher 2007
        Microsoft Office Word 2007
        Microsoft Office Tools
            Digital Certificate for VBA Projects
            Microsoft Clip Organizer
```

Figure 40.9
Microsoft Office Tools.

6 Type the name of your certificate in the Create Digital Certificate dialogue box, as shown in Figure 40.10.

7 When you click OK, you will see the SelfCert Success dialogue box, as shown in Figure 40.11.

8 Click OK.

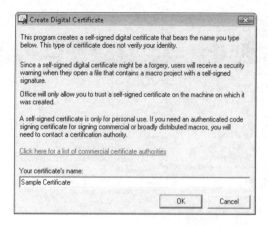

Figure 40.10
Add a certificate name.

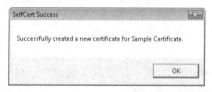

Figure 40.11
SelfCert Success dialogue box.

Follow these steps to create a signed package:

1 Click the Microsoft Office Button while you are in the database that will be packaged and signed.

2 Select Publish. Click **Package and Sign**.

3 In the Select Certificate dialogue box, choose the appropriate certificate. Click **OK**.

4 Locate and select the location of the signed database package in Create Microsoft Office Access Signed Package, as shown in Figure 40.12.

40

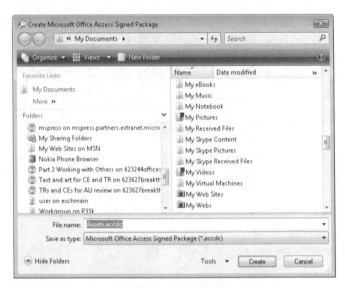

Figure 40.12
Select the location of the signed database package.

5 In the **File Name** box, locate and choose the location of the signed database package.

6 Click **Create**.

After creating the .accde file, Access will place it into your preferred location.

Important

Each package can include only one database.

brilliant
pocket books

The ultimate pocket sized guides to the new Windows Vista and Office 2007

brilliant pocket books – the fast answer